utb 6028

D1699356

Eine Arbeitsgemeinschaft der Verlage

Brill | Schöningh – Fink · Paderborn
Brill | Vandenhoeck & Ruprecht · Göttingen – Böhlau · Wien · Köln
Verlag Barbara Budrich · Opladen · Toronto
facultas · Wien
Haupt Verlag · Bern
Verlag Julius Klinkhardt · Bad Heilbrunn
Mohr Siebeck · Tübingen
Narr Francke Attempto Verlag – expert verlag · Tübingen
Psychiatrie Verlag · Köln
Ernst Reinhardt Verlag · München
transcript Verlag · Bielefeld
Verlag Eugen Ulmer · Stuttgart
UVK Verlag · München
Waxmann · Münster · New York
wbv Publikation · Bielefeld
Wochenschau Verlag · Frankfurt am Main

Gerlinde Mautner is a Full Professor of English Business Communication at WU, the Vienna University of Economics and Business. She has many years of experience in teaching advanced linguistic skills and English academic writing both to faculty and to students from the undergraduate to the doctoral level. The focus of her research is on the relationship between language and society, as well as on questions of methodology. She has published widely in high-impact outlets and acts as a reviewer for several international journals.

Christopher J. Ross is an experienced writer, translator, and text editor specialising in research articles and books. He was a Senior Lecturer at WU for nearly 20 years, having previously held the same post at the Department of Interpreting and Translating, Heriot-Watt University (Edinburgh).

Studieren, aber richtig
Herausgegeben von Michael Huter, Huter & Roth, Wien

Die Bände behandeln jeweils ein Bündel von Fähigkeiten und Fertigkeiten. Das gesamte Paket versetzt Studierende in die Lage, die wesentlichen Aufgaben im Studium zu erfüllen. Die Themen orientieren sich an den wichtigsten Situationen und Formen des Wissenserwerbs. Dabei werden auch das scheinbar Selbstverständliche behandelt und die Zusammenhänge erklärt.

Weitere Bände:
Otto Kruse: Lesen und Schreiben (utb 3355)
Klaus Niedermair: Recherchieren und Dokumentieren (utb 3356)
Theo Hug, Gerald Poscheschnik: Empirisch Forschen (utb 3357)
Gerlinde Mautner: Wissenschaftliches Englisch (utb 3444)
Jasmin Bastian, Lena Groß: Lernen und Wissen (utb 3779)
Melanie Moll, Winfried Thielmann: Wissenschaftliches Deutsch (utb 4650)
Otto Kruse: Kritisches Denken und Argumentieren (utb 4767)
Sabine Dengscherz, Michèle Cooke: Transkulturelle Kommunikation (utb 5319)
Steffen-Peter Ballstaedt: Wissenschaftliche Bilder: gut gestalten, richtig verwenden (utb 6031)

Gerlinde Mautner / Christopher J. Ross

English Academic Writing

A Guide for the Humanities and Social Sciences

UVK Verlag · München

Umschlagmotiv: © shutterstock.com

Bibliografische Information der Deutschen Nationalbibliothek
Die Deutsche Nationalbibliothek verzeichnet diese Publikation in der Deutschen
Nationalbibliografie; detaillierte bibliografische Daten sind im Internet über
http://dnb.dnb.de abrufbar.

DOI: https://doi.org/10.36198/9783838560281

© UVK Verlag 2023
– ein Unternehmen der Narr Francke Attempto Verlag GmbH + Co. KG
Dischingerweg 5 · D-72070 Tübingen

Internet: www.narr.de
eMail: info@narr.de

Einbandgestaltung: siegel konzeption | gestaltung
CPI books GmbH, Leck

utb-Nr. 6028
ISBN 978-3-8252-6028-6 (Print)
ISBN 978-3-8385-6028-1 (ePDF)
ISBN 978-3-8463-6028-6 (ePub)

Contents

Acknowledgments

We would like to express our sincere thanks to the following:

- Daniel Green, for his support in preparing the final manuscript;
- Christina Drimmel, for once again being on hand whenever MS Word displayed its temperamental side, or our own lack of IT competence was exposed.

Explanatory notes for readers

Welcome to *English Academic Writing*. The following notes sum up a number of editorial decisions we took in writing this book.

- As its subtitle suggests, our book is aimed primarily at researchers in the humanities and social sciences, where our own backgrounds lie. However, we are confident that academics from the life sciences and natural sciences will also find much here that is useful to them.
- While our approach is largely *descriptive* of existing good practice, illustrated by numerous authentic examples, we do not shy away from being *prescriptive* when it seems appropriate. What we have sought hard to avoid, however, are unwarranted generalisations and finger-wagging instructions.
- All chapters include a brief introduction, including a *What's coming up* box indicating the division into sections and subsections.
- They conclude with a bulleted summary of the main 'takeaways'. These lists are intended only as brief reminders. They will make little sense if you have not previously read the relevant part of the chapter in question.
- Within the chapters, you will find two types of summary box:
  - □ *Toolboxes*, which contain linguistic tips of various kinds
  - □ *In Brief* boxes with compact summaries of a particular issue
- You will also find some *Makeovers*. These illustrate a particular point by showing how flaws in an (invented) short text – the *Before* version – can be corrected by using the techniques described in the section concerned to create an improved *After* version.
- You can, if you wish, use the *Makeovers* as exercises; this would mean writing your own *After* version before you look at the one provided. Please note that there is absolutely no suggestion that our revised version is the only 'right answer'; it merely provides an illustration of how the problems in the *Before* section might be addressed.
- The extracts are all authentic examples drawn from articles or books published by reputable outlets. We have made no changes to the extracts apart from those mentioned in the next point. Italicisation is as in the original texts and, in order to preserve the academic character of these, we have also left all footnote numbers in.

- We have made some minor changes to the extracts, always with the utmost care to avoid any possible distortion of the original. Specifically, we have:
  - □ emboldened particular words and longer stretches of language to highlight the linguistic point being illustrated
  - □ indicated explicitly any emboldening already present in the original of an extract
  - □ omitted passages essential neither to the original message nor to the linguistic point being illustrated (such omissions are indicated by [...])
  - □ added short explanations where the lack of context makes them necessary (e.g., *she* [Julie Smith])
- However, in Chapter 6 (Citations) we have not emboldened entire citations within extracts, as this could have been misleading for readers. Purely linguistic points (e.g., verb tenses, examples of reporting verbs) are emboldened as elsewhere.
- Contrary to normal citation practice, source references for the extracts are given above the text, immediately following the extract number and in square brackets (e.g., [Hofmann 2020: 56]). We have done this to avoid possible confusion in cases where the extract itself ends with a source reference.
- Examples in the running text, whether authentic or invented, are italicised.
- Examples showing bad practice or including grammatical errors have an asterisk (*) placed in front of them.
- If you wish to read more about the topic of English academic writing, you may find the following titles useful: Booth et al. (2016), Macgilchrist (2014), Pollock (2021), Siepmann et al. (2022), Swales & Feak (2012), Sword (2012) and Turabian (2018). Full details can be found in our *List of references*. Some readers may be surprised not to see Strunk & White ([1918] 1999) among our recommended sources. The omission is deliberate, for the reasons set out in Pullum (2009, 2010).

Introduction:
Seven pillars of academic writing

Wisdom has built her house,
She has hewn out her seven pillars.
(Proverbs 9:1)

The American writer Kurt Vonnegut is famous above all for his novels; less well known are his observations on how to write. One of his key messages is "pity the readers" (Vonnegut 1981: 67; Vonnegut & McConnell 2019). Although Vonnegut does not deal specifically with academic writing, his appeal will resonate with everyone who has on occasion found research publications a challenge to read. Too often that challenge arises not because the content is complex, but because it is expressed in unnecessarily complicated language. If, on the other hand, a writer chooses language so as to support readers, then his or her ideas and arguments are more likely to make the desired impression. Importantly, these choices affect language on all levels, ranging from words and sentence structures to the organisation of whole texts.

It is this link between linguistic choices and concern for the reader that forms the basis of the approach pursued here. Our book is inspired by "a view of writing as a social and communicative engagement between writer and reader" (Hyland & Tse 2004: 156). For the two sides to engage successfully, English research writing must display certain features which are widely regarded as essential.

We have picked seven of these features, which we have dubbed *seven pillars* of academic writing, and we will discuss them in the seven chapters of this book. They are as follows:

1. Well-planned, clearly structured **texts** with a strong narrative feel
2. Well-designed **paragraphs** each of which introduces, develops and rounds off a single main idea
3. Well-constructed **sentences** that flow naturally and focus on their final element
4. Pro-active **punctuation** that shows readers where best to pause for breath

5. Helpful **cohesion** that verbalises the connections between the elements of paragraphs and of the whole text
6. Appropriate **citations** which underpin the writer's arguments with the words and ideas of other authors
7. **Guidance and persuasion** that nudge the reader towards accepting the writer's case

Taken together, the seven pillars enable academic writing to be made effective, reader-friendly and appealing, without accepting any compromises on substance, rigour and precision. The quality of the underlying research and the quality of the writing go hand in hand. If the latter doesn't sparkle, then neither will the former. Conversely, no amount of stylistic brilliance can rescue a flawed research design. Yet, even if we will occasionally touch upon such notions as research paradigms, epistemology and methodology, these cannot be our concern here. Instead, our book aims to provide academics in the humanities and social sciences with guidance about putting their ideas down 'on paper' clearly, succinctly, convincingly, and in a way that will appeal to their readers. In short, this book will not teach you about *doing* research, but about *writing* it *up.*

In organising your work flow, however, it can be counterproductive to treat the two activities as completely separate processes to be carried out one after another. Instead of saying 'I've done all the research and all I need to do now is write it up', you may find it helpful to start writing as soon as you possibly can, about whichever parts of the research you have already (semi-)completed. Certainly that means there will editing and re-writing to do later, but that would have been the case anyway. The key point is that writing your ideas down forces you to formulate them clearly, enabling you to spot weaknesses in your argument and areas where you need to do some more targeted reading and thinking. And it is a lot better to discover such things early on, well before the deadline for submission is looming.

Before we move on to the body of the book, a brief but important disclaimer about the status of English as an international language of research. Its significance is beyond doubt, and if you didn't agree, you wouldn't have bought or borrowed this book. Does it follow that the dominance of English is universal, or that this development is unequivocally positive? No, to both questions. In some disciplines, knowledge of languages other than English remains essential, especially when it comes to reading and interpreting source texts from a variety of cultures. And it cannot be denied that the seemingly inexorable spread of English has led to many national languages effectively losing their capacity and status as languages of research. However, neither us writing this book nor you reading it should be construed as signalling approval of this state of affairs: acquiescence perhaps, even if it is only along the lines of 'If you can't beat 'em, join 'em'.

Needless to say, we very much hope it is not merely out of a sense of resignation that you have picked up this book. The measure of our success as writers will be whether we manage to impress upon you our own enthusiasm for academic writing; for the exciting challenge of sharing one's research with others; and for the power of the English language to tell a good story.

1 *Creativity and constraints*: Planning research texts

> *"Begin at the beginning," the King said,*
> *very gravely, "and go on till you*
> *come to the end: then stop."*
> LEWIS CARROLL (1832 – 1898),
> *Alice in Wonderland*

The first of the pillars on which a good research publication rests is a well-planned structure. As a writer, you have considerable freedom to devise your own. However, you must do so within certain constraints (as in the concept of 'freedom under the rule of law'). To quote Pollock (2021: 3), in every form of writing "the creativity comes from successfully conveying what you want within the bounds of the form".

By 'form', Pollock is referring to what linguists call *genre*. A genre is a type of text (spoken or written) for which society, or a part of it, has developed generally accepted conventions, relating among other things to text structure. Having been created by group consensus, genres can only be changed consensually, not single-handedly by individuals. They are therefore restrictive, but they are also liberating in that they take some responsibility off the academic writer's shoulders. You can be certain that, if you comply with your discipline's genre conventions, your writing will be accepted as a valid contribution to the field. People may still disagree with it, of course, but within the boundaries of the genre they will at least know how to engage with you.

Following the constraints imposed by the relevant genres thus helps you write texts that your peers accept as legitimate. But that is hardly an ambitious goal. Nor will achieving it be sufficient to make your texts stand out from the crowd. If you aim to do that, you may find it helpful to conceive of your research text as a narrative, as a 'research story'. Indeed, Pollock's (2021: 1) advice – "Think like a storyteller" – reflects a widespread strand of thinking. The metaphor is so powerful because it appeals to our sense of narrative as an ancient, deeply ingrained social practice. It imposes certain structural constraints, true, but these are of a fairly general nature: for example, the need for an identifiable beginning and ending, and for some form of narrative development. A sense of progress needs to be created by moving from some form of problem to its eventual resolution. Framed like this, research texts move up that significant notch from interesting to fascinating, and the act of research writing emerges as both rule-bound and creative.

Nonetheless, research 'story-telling' is not about rhetorical grandstanding, or style without substance. It is simply about ensuring that the text appeals to its audience, so that readers become fully engaged and ready to share the writer's enthusiasm for the topic. Exactly how that works is difficult to pin down because text appeal derives from a whole range of features. Some are situated specifically on the paragraph and sentence levels, and we will discuss them in Sections 2.3 and 3.4, respectively. More generally, text appeal depends on a myriad of specific, micro-level linguistic choices that will keep us busy for the rest of the book. In this chapter, though, our focus will be firmly on the macro level of textual structure.

WHAT'S COMING UP

1.1 Research genres

Academic writing is frequently discussed in terms of 'genre' (Swales 1990, 2004). Genres share certain communicative purposes and formal characteristics that readers have come to expect. Meeting their expectations enables writers to take part in the key conversations in their field and to gain access to the relevant research community.

In the context of research writing, the most common genres are journal articles, edited volumes and monographs (i.e., books on a single subject). Each of them has its own conventions, which in some cases also differ between disciplines. These 'rules' place restrictions on writers' freedom to decide on text structure: for example, through the widespread practices of including an abstract or of bookending an argument with an introduction and a conclusion. Other structural conventions (e.g., including a section on theory) may be less universal, but still relevant across many different disciplines and different text types. In this section, we will look more closely at how and why genres matter so much, before going into more detail about both the restrictions they impose and the creative opportunities they can open up.

1.1.1 Genres, structures and hierarchies

Genres matter to writers above all because they matter to readers. In fact, observing such genre conventions is the first act of the 'pity' towards the reader that we declared in the Introduction to be the basis of all (research) writing. The importance of a genre label for readers is that it acts like a set of instructions for navigating and interpreting the text. It triggers certain expectations in the reader's mind: expectations about the nature of the content, structure, layout and style.

Conversely, genres also raise expectations about what will *not* appear in a text. In particular, readers of a research text will not expect to encounter digressions from the main line of argument (known in German as *Exkurse*). Significantly, English does not even have a name for what in other writing cultures is quite a popular subgenre (in English, the word *excursus* exists but is rarely if ever used). As Clyne (1987: 213-214) explains: "The *Exkurs* has neither a conceptual equivalent nor a translation equivalent in English." That may change, of course, as and when English becomes established as 'the' language of research across even more cultures and disciplines. For the moment, however, academic writing in English presents you with a stark choice. If a point is central enough to be made at all, it needs to be properly integrated into the body of the text; if it is only peripheral, it will be considered an unwelcome distraction which should not be there at all.

Having been raised, expectations must be met. If the reader is an expert called upon to evaluate the text – in their capacity as a supervisor, editor or reviewer – the genre label acts as a frame of reference that defines the standard of assessment. Which brings us full circle back to the writer. For by choosing a particular genre label for their text they have it in their power to influence the judgement of the expert reader. This is why it is important, for example, to submit journal articles in the right category, be it 'review article', 'theoretical' or 'empirical'.

A second reason why genres matter to the aspiring academic is that they mediate access and participation at various points along the way. In the early stages, bachelor's and master's theses mark the passage from undergraduate to graduate and from the latter to a first salaried position. Further on, the doctoral thesis acts as the gatekeeper to promotion (or, to the cynically inclined, as an initiation rite). The thesis quality-stamps not only the fledgling researcher's grasp of key concepts and methods, but also their ability to share findings in a manner that is widely recognised and respected. That said, it would make little sense for us to generalise about genres linked to academic degrees, since the rules governing them are partly laid down and enforced by the degree-awarding institution. Instead, we will focus on the genres policed by the academic community at large.

Once the researcher has successfully embarked on an academic career, they will begin to use a multitude of such genres, ranging from the very brief and informal (e.g., e-mails about a collaborative grant application) to highly formal and elaborate examples such as monographs and edited collections. Increasingly relevant across disciplines are genres that reach out to the wider community such as blogs, TV interviews and contributions to public panel discussions. Moreover, as researchers are now expected to bid for competitive funding, the genre of the grant proposal has also acquired general importance (see Appendix 2). Apart from that, the genres that are most common and prestigious vary between disciplines. Whereas in the life sciences original research is published almost exclusively in journals, many humanities disciplines continue to treasure the monograph and chapters in edited volumes.

During their formative years, researchers pick up their discipline's various genre conventions through implicit socialisation and explicit training. Such rules relate not only to generating new knowledge, but also to communicating that knowledge in various settings. For example, new researchers learn what a journal article must look like to be accepted as a legitimate contribution.

Sometimes the genre rules can be very specific, an example being the so-called AIMRaD structure. The acronym consists of the initials for *Abstract, Introduction, Methods, Results and Discussion.* The actual titles of the sections may vary, of course, and writers are free to include subsections. Developed originally in the natural sciences, AIMRaD has now also become a standard pattern for empirical research papers in most of the social sciences and some of the humanities. Still, it is clearly not *de rigueur* in all disciplines. If you browse humanities journals, you will find any number of papers that do not adhere to the AIMRaD template. (To find out whether the pattern applies to your own research, it's best to have a look at a range of papers from your field's top journals.)

What is universally accepted is that written-up research must be organised systematically, in a structure that is familiar to the relevant community, laid down by the genre conventions and generally hierarchical in nature. There is such a variety of structures that it would have been hopelessly overambitious – and ultimately not very helpful for the reader – to try and provide detailed, discipline-specific instructions for all genres. We have therefore gone for a two-step approach that transcends both discipline and genre. First, in the next subsection, we will explain how a hierarchy can be a very helpful way of organising research texts. Then, in Section 1.2, we will turn to the perspective that views research writing as a form of 'story'.

In Brief
THE IMPORTANCE OF GENRES FOR RESEARCH WRITING

- Genre conventions constrain text structure in the interests of both readers and writers.
- Respecting genre conventions assists researchers in having their voices heard within their disciplinary community.
- Genre conventions may vary widely from one discipline to another.
- In general, research genres require texts to have a hierarchical structure of some sort.

1.1.2 Hierarchical organisation in research texts

What do we mean by organising research texts as hierarchies? We mean that the various elements into which a text is divided are arranged on a series of different levels, and that the elements on one level are subordinate to those on the level above. The hierarchy can be made apparent to readers in a range of different ways. At the 'strict' end of the spectrum, section headings are numbered (1, 2, 3, ...), as are their subsections (1.1, 1.2, ...; 2.1, ...) and possibly also the subdivisions of these (1.1.1, 1.1.2, ...; 1.2.1, ...). In addition, the headings may be distinguished by the use of different fonts. At the 'loose' end, these latter will be the only indication of hierarchy. In fact, few hierarchically organised articles seem to include more than two levels, while in the case of a book, chapters will form an additional tier right at the top.

Making your thoughts fit this general mould is undoubtedly a constraint, but doing so is very beneficial for your readers. It enables them to find their way easily through the text, it means they do not have to guess what belongs where, and it allows them to concentrate on content without being distracted by structural flaws. And, as ever, anything that helps your readers will help to get your message across.

Headings and hierarchy

Headings – how they are worded, that is – play a crucial role in making hierarchy transparent. Ideally, the headings of units at one level should 'nest' into their hierarchical superior (in the case of the highest-level units, into the title of the article or book); that is, every heading should indicate that the unit's content constitutes a subset of the superior unit's content. In that sense, the whole structure would be like a set of Russian *matryoshka* dolls. On the other hand, headings on the same level ought to have parallel grammatical structures, yet indicate clearly distinctive content. Regularly checking your table of contents (e.g., by using the 'Headline' function in MS Word) will help to ensure that you adhere to these principles.

A particularly scrupulous example is to be found in Sofaer et al. (2021), an article from the field of heritage studies. We have set out the main features of the hierarchical arrangement it uses in the following table.

Level	Title/heading		
Article	*Heritage site, value and wellbeing: learning from the COVID-19 pandemic in England*		
Section	*Places of joy: heritage after lockdown*	*Visits to heritage sites and wellbeing values*	*Translating heritage site visitor values to wellbeing outcomes*
Subsection		*Heritage visits and ...* ■ *notions of capability* ■ *social connections* ■ *ontological security* ■ *trust*	■ *Hedonic wellbeing* ■ *Eudaimonic wellbeing*

Table 1.1. Title nesting and parallelism
Source: Sofaer et al. (2021)[1]

In this case, nesting is achieved at the section level through repetition of four key terms appearing in the title (*heritage, site(s), wellbeing* and *values*) as well as the indirect reference to *pandemic* by means of *lockdown*. In the second section, *heritage visits* is repeated at the start of all the subsection titles, which then continue with an example of *wellbeing values*. In the third section, the *wellbeing* in its title is repeated in both headings at the lower level. Meanwhile, parallelism is ensured by the use of noun phrases throughout all levels, with the sole exception of the third section title, where the noun phrase begins with an -*ing* form (technically, a gerund). At first glance, this change in grammatical pattern might seem to slightly reduce the powerful structuring effect. But it actually serves an important narrative purpose by signalling a move away from *describing* empirical findings to *discussing* them.

1.2 The research story and its parts

We turn now to a completely different way of thinking about research texts: seeing them as 'research stories'. When we think of stories, it is unlikely that research publications spring immediately to mind. Instead, we will probably

---

[1]   The table does not include the *Introduction* and *Conclusion* sections because neither has any subsections. Similarly, the first section included in the table (*Places of joy ...*) is not subdivided.

think of the tales in *1001 Nights* or novels such as *The Name of the Rose* or *The Lord of the Rings*: fictional narratives that are the products of the writer's imagination and appeal to that of the reader. Research, by contrast, is all about constructing an argument on the basis of evidence.

Thus, clearly, *research story* is merely a metaphor and cannot possibly reflect all aspects of research texts. Later on, we will have occasion to remark on points at which the metaphor breaks down (as metaphors tend to do if you stretch them too far): points, that is, where such texts are not at all like stories in the usual sense. Yet, even so, the image highlights important qualities of academic writing, such as the need to capture and hold readers' attention, to guide them through the text, and to maintain a sense of progress in moving towards a conclusion – in other words, to give them a good read, an idea we will return to in Section 1.3.

At the most basic level, the story metaphor indicates that research texts need to have three identifiable parts: a beginning, a middle and an end. In the following subsections, we will examine these parts of the research story in turn. Given the diversity of the humanities and social sciences, with their plethora of theories, methods and genres, not to mention the different types of journal articles (theoretical and empirical, quantitative and qualitative), it would be impossible to stipulate exactly what will come in each part. Specifying precise section names across the board is out of the question. What we are confident we can do is to outline the *function* carried out by each of the story's three parts, as well as what is needed to fulfil that function. First, though, we must make a brief detour to discuss a part of journal papers which stands at the beginning yet outside the story itself: the abstract.

1.2.1 The abstract

An abstract is a compact and self-contained text – hence our decision to deal with it separately – yet it is obviously twinned with the research story to be developed properly in the paper itself. In fact, it is a miniature version of that story. As a publisher's website explains: "An abstract is a succinct summary of a larger piece of work that aims to persuade readers to read the full document – essentially, it acts as a shop window, enticing people to step inside."[2]

---

2   https://www.emeraldgrouppublishing.com/how-to/authoring-editing-reviewing/write-article-abstract, accessed 26 July 2022

Abstracts are a typical, though not universal feature of journal articles (and of submissions to academic conferences). They may not be the most exciting texts to write. Yet Belcher's (2019: 92-93) list of their key functions – "connecting with editors", "connecting with peer reviewers", "getting found", "getting read" and "getting cited" – indicates clearly why it is worthwhile spending a fair amount of time and effort on getting your abstract right. For the stakes are high. A compelling abstract may sway a journal editor into sending your paper out to review rather than desk-rejecting it, and a researcher into agreeing to do the review rather than declining. It may also be the abstract that attracts the attention of someone searching the web and encourages them to read the full article. Over and above that, writing an abstract can assist writers as "a diagnostic tool" highlighting problems in their main text. "If you can't write a brief abstract of your article", Belcher remarks, "then your article may lack focus" (p. 92). In that case, it will not be the abstract that needs revising but the paper.

Now for some technical details relating to abstracts. First, in journal articles they are placed between the paper's title and the start of the introduction, so technically in a space that lies outside the paper proper. This special status is significant because, as we will see later, it justifies a different approach to citation. It also means that some repetition is tolerated between the abstract and the body of the paper. Second, abstracts vary in length, depending on the discipline and the publication outlet; in the humanities and social sciences, they typically range from about 150 to 300 words. These limits are set by publishers, editors and conference organisers, so authors usually have no say in the matter. Basically, you do as you're told. Third, most journals also require you to supply a set of keywords which are typically printed right underneath the abstract or alongside it. Apart from facilitating online searches, keywords also help editors to identify reviewers whose expertise matches the paper's topic, theory and method. As that fit is essential, authors should choose their keywords wisely.

The opening sentence

Given that the function of abstracts is to 'entice readers to step inside', it is hardly surprising that the first sentence plays a special role. There are two basic approaches to writing it. One is to resort to what later in this book will be introduced as a metacomment (see 7.1), using phrases such as *This paper discusses*. The following are typical examples.

TYPICAL OPENING SENTENCES FROM ABSTRACTS

Extract 1.1 [Jones, H. 2019: 187]

This paper is concerned with how law organises and controls space.

Extract 1.2 [Coffey & Leung 2019: 607]

In this paper we investigate the ways in which creativity is understood and enacted by language teachers.

Extract 1.3 [Levy 2020: 1]

This survey synthesizes and examines existing scholarship on women's practices and positions within eighteenth century British book culture.

The second, and arguably more elegant approach is to formulate a statement that introduces the topic in fairly broad, even non-technical terms, giving a diverse readership a general idea of what the paper is about. Importantly, such an opening sentence usually avoids tackling controversial points head-on. Instead, it is more likely to be "a general, relatively uncontentious statement" (Murray & Moore 2006: 59). Extracts 1.4 to 1.6 – all of them from highly specialised scholarly journals – provide fairly typical examples.

"UNCONTENTIOUS STATEMENTS" INTRODUCING ABSTRACTS

Extract 1.4 [Taylor 2020: 171]

Social categories play a central role in inquiry.

Extract 1.5 [Fleming 2021: 1]

Incumbent prime ministers who win re-election often reshuffle their cabinet ministers.

Extract 1.6 [Howlett 2022: 387]

For many social science scholars, the COVID-19 pandemic has forced us to re-think our approaches to research.

A very general first sentence is particularly useful if you cannot be entirely sure who your readers will be. Given the nature of research papers, there is generally little doubt that your audience will primarily consist of other researchers, and often very senior ones, but this does not necessarily mean that they will be specialists in your precise area. And, should they not be, keeping the jargon less than 'full on' at the outset will make it easier to entice them in.

Content

As regards structure and content, Swales (1990: 179) puts it in a nutshell. "The essence of the genre", he explains, "is one of distillation". The 'distilling' results in what is effectively "a fully self-contained, capsule description of the paper" (Koopman 1997), with the latter's main sections represented in the abstract. This is well illustrated in Extract 1.7, which is drawn from a paper structured strictly on AIMRaD lines (with its constituent sections numbered 1 to 4 and headed *Introduction, Materials and Methods, Findings* and *Discussion*). As is readily apparent from the abstract, these are reflected almost exactly in the sequence of its sentences (in Extracts 1.7 and 1.8, sentence numbers have been added as a basis for Table 1.2 and our discussion of it).

ABSTRACT REFLECTING AIMRaD STRUCTURE

Extract 1.7 [Thomas 2021: 693]

[1]While disability has historically been depicted in problematic ways in television, film, and print media, more balanced and progressive cultural representations are arguably emerging. [2]However, few studies address how disabled people and their families (e.g., parents) encounter, and make sense of, media configurations ostensibly designed to promote a more positive and visible image of living with disability. [3]Drawing upon interviews with parents of children with Down's syndrome in the United Kingdom, I sketch out how they feel about depictions that, arguably, depart from hurtful historical narratives of disability as tragic and pitiable. [4]Parents praise, and mostly embrace, recent portrayals of people with Down's syndrome in media outputs. [5]At the same time, they raise concerns around tokenism, stereotyping, focusing upon "exceptional" people, and fueling sanitized accounts which deny, or at least obscure, the harsh lived realities for many parents of disabled children. [6]I conclude by arguing that while parents largely applaud and welcome positive public narratives, they also fear that such representations threaten to gloss over the pervasive mistreatment, disregard, and disenfranchisement of disabled people and their families.

Even if a paper does not follow a template as rigid as AIMRaD, the headings of its various sections and subsections – provided they have been well-chosen – can form an excellent basis for its abstract. In Extract 1.8, for example, virtually the entire abstract text is made up of such components.

ANOTHER WELL-STRUCTURED ABSTRACT

Extract 1.8 [Moore et al. 2017: 1]

[1]The rhetoric of "excellence" is pervasive across the academy. [2]It is used to refer to research outputs as well as researchers, theory and education, individuals and organizations, from art history to zoology. [3]But does "excellence" actually mean anything? [4]Does this pervasive narrative of "excellence" do any good? [5]Drawing on a range of sources we interrogate "excellence" as a concept and find that it has no intrinsic meaning in academia. [6]Rather it functions as a linguistic interchange mechanism. [7]To investigate whether this linguistic function is useful we examine how the rhetoric of excellence combines with narratives of scarcity and competition to show that the hyper-competition that arises from the performance of "excellence" is completely at odds with the qualities of good research. [8]We trace the roots of issues in reproducibility, fraud, and homophily to this rhetoric. [9]But we also show that this rhetoric is an internal, and not primarily an external, imposition. [10]We conclude by proposing an alternative rhetoric based on soundness and capacity-building. [11]In the final analysis, it turns out that that "excellence" is not excellent. [12]Used in its current unqualified form it is a pernicious and dangerous rhetoric that undermines the very foundations of good research and scholarship. [13]This article is published as part of a collection on the future of research assessment.

Naturally, not all abstracts can be constructed in this way. But whether they are or not, they should always contain certain key elements. To ensure they are all there, Koopman (1997) recommends using the following checklist:

Motivation: Why do we care about the problem and the results?
Problem statement: What problem are you trying to solve?
Approach: How did you go about solving or making progress on the problem?
Results: What's the answer?
Conclusions: What are the implications of your answer?

He suggests that each of these points is generally reflected in a single sentence of the abstract, but also points out that "the parts may be merged or spread among a set of sentences". In Table 1.2, we indicate where each of them is located in the examples above.

	Extract 1.7	**Extract 1.8**
Motivation	Sentences 1 & 2	Sentences 1, 2 & 13
Problem statement	Sentence 2	Sentences 3 & 4
Approach	Sentence 3	Sentences 5 & 7
Results	Sentences 4 & 5	Sentences 5, 6, 8 & 9
Conclusion	Sentence 6	Sentences 10, 11 & 12

Table 1.2. Koopman's (1997) checklist applied to Extracts 1.7 and 1.8

What about the language of abstracts? Regardless of the abstract's opening sentence, from the second sentence onward the terminology of your topic area will certainly be prominently represented (out of necessity, but also to confirm your credentials as a subject expert). This is again well illustrated in our two examples. In Extract 1.7, *disability/disabled, Down's syndrome* and *media* all feature at least twice, while the term *media configurations* is echoed in *representations, depictions* and *portrayals*. In Extract 1.8, the key terms are *"excellence"*, with quote marks as shown (seven appearances and one echo in *excellent*), *rhetoric* (six appearances) and *research*, which appears three times but is also echoed in *researchers, scholarship, the academy* and *academia*.

Also notable are the considerable efforts made by both authors to observe the general principles of paragraph design (see Chapter 2) and cohesion (Chapter 5). In spite of the strict word limit, there are a number of linking expressions (e.g., *rather; as we also show; in doing so; in relation to the former*), and there is variation in sentence structures, including their beginnings. Thus, although abstracts may not be the place to display great creativity, there is no question that well-written specimens observe exactly the same principles as the longer genres they are related to.

There is one exception, however. Unlike other research genres, abstracts need not – some say must not – contain source references. Word-for-word citations in particular are extremely rare; if they *are* used, then quotation marks and source references must of course be included so as not to inadvertently commit plagiarism. But generally, the understanding is that the absence of sources in the abstract does not amount to a claim on the part of the author that the ideas expressed are all original. It simply means that readers will have to wait for source references until they get to the actual paper.

Structured abstracts

The examples we have seen so far, both of which were written as single paragraphs, are what one might call *standard abstracts*. That is because there is an alternative format that some publishers and funding organisations have made compulsory. It is known as a *structured abstract* (rather a misnomer, given that a good standard abstract is also 'structured').

A structured abstract in the narrower sense is one split up into sections with headlines that are set down by the publisher or funder and cannot be changed by the author. The precise wording of the headlines may differ from journal to journal, but the overall structure will be very similar. If you want to submit a paper to any of the journals published by Emerald, for example, you'll have to fill in the following four obligatory fields: *purpose; design/methodology/approach; findings* and *originality/value*. Another three are optional, though they may be required by some Emerald journals: *research limitations/implications; practical implications; social implications*.[3] Here is an example, from a paper entitled *Drivers of growth expectations in Latin American rural contexts.*

A STRUCTURED ABSTRACT

Extract 1.9 [Mahn et al. 2022: n. pag.; original emboldening][4]
Purpose – Given the importance of growth-oriented entrepreneurship in the context of economic development and the need to understand how rural communities can be developed, the purpose of this research paper is to determine how the drivers of growth expectations differ between urban and rural settings.

---

3   https://www.emeraldgrouppublishing.com/how-to/authoring-editing-reviewing/writ e-article-abstract, accessed 27 July 2022

4   This particular structured abstract also contains sections headed *Keywords* and *Paper type*, but we have omitted them because they are not a feature of structured abstracts *per se*; not all such abstracts include them, and they may also appear, in some form, in standard ones.

Design/methodology/approach – The methodology is threefold: firstly, a descriptive analysis with nonparametric testing is conducted; then [a] pooled regression model is used to analyse the predictors of growth expectations in both contexts, and finally, coarsened exact matching is used to identify possible self-selection bias.

Findings – In contrast to mainstream entrepreneurship theory, it is found that entrepreneurs' intrinsic knowledge, skills and abilities are not significant in the rural-specific model. The only exception is entrepreneurs' educational level, the importance of which is emphasised as a pivotal factor in increasing high-growth ventures in rural communities. Additionally, when self-selection is eliminated, rurality worsens growth intentions.

Practical implications – There is evidence that some growth-oriented entrepreneurs self-select into rural communities. Because the high-growth entrepreneurial dynamics in rural areas are unique, public policies should target purpose-driven entrepreneurial education. This includes encouraging "lifestyle entrepreneurship" (e.g. retirees returning to rural areas to become entrepreneurs), preventing entrepreneurial brain drain in rural areas and attracting highly educated urban entrepreneurs to exploit opportunities in rural areas.

Originality/value – This research attempts to contribute to the ongoing debate regarding the factors that drive high-growth entrepreneurs in rural areas by analysing rural entrepreneurs in the high-growth context of a developing economy. The focus is on Chile – a country that is rarely investigated compared to the USA or Europe – to extend the literature on high-growth ventures and entrepreneurial ecosystems.

The fixed headlines in structured abstracts may feel like a straitjacket at first; but, on the other hand, the rigid structure ensures that no essential element is left out. Another plus is that one has to worry less about cohesion and flow; nonetheless, it is notable that the authors of our example have included a number of cohesive devices (*given the importance of; threefold, firstly, then, and finally; in contrast to; additionally; because; this includes*). From the reader's perspective, structured abstracts are unequivocally good news: not only because they are faster to read, but also because the reader can make a beeline for precisely the information they are looking for, such as the methods used.

In Brief
ABSTRACTS

- An abstract is a key element of a research article since it draws readers in and provides 'visibility'.
- It constitutes a 'pocket version' of the article as whole.
- The first sentence is crucial.
- The abstract should include the article's main points and the key terms it uses.
- It may take the form of a so-called structured abstract with fixed headings.

1.2.2 The beginning: Setting the scene

Returning to the story proper, we will follow the advice in the quote at the head of this chapter and begin at the beginning: that is, the part of the story in which the scene is set for the main action to follow. As already mentioned, this is done by delineating a problem or puzzle – Aristotle called this 'tying a knot' – that will be addressed and resolved ('untied') in the remaining two parts. Although the most common place to do this is in an introduction, the beginning in our sense can involve more than that. In fact it will do so, since the scene-setting starts even before the story itself does – with the title you choose to give it.

Titles

Giving a story an effective title is central to its chances of success – and a great opportunity for some creative thinking. For titles need to be appealing (i.e., easily comprehensible and inviting), and they work best if they are succinct (short and to the point, but not cryptically so). In the case of a journal paper, though, that alone will not suffice. As a widely-used style guide states, an effective title should include "essential terms [...] that clarify the topic of your paper for readers" (American Psychological Association 2020: 7). Just how many such terms are advisable depends on the nature of the journal to which an article is submitted. If it is a highly specialist one, aimed at a relatively small and homogeneous audience, then readers will want to know exactly which part of the field is discussed. If the journal covers a broad field, then similar considerations will apply as to the first sentence of an abstract (see previous subsection) and it will probably be better to go easy on the jargon.

Within these limits, a range of syntactic variants is possible. Here we offer a number of options without excluding the possibility, even likelihood of others that are just as acceptable. The first option is to split a title into two parts separated by a colon, as is shown by these two examples.[5]

TWO-PART TITLES
Extract 1.10 [Donaldson, Ward & Bradley 2010: 1521]
Mess among disciplines: interdisciplinarity in environmental research

Extract 1.11 [Haire & MacDonald 2019: 273]
Humour in music therapy: A narrative literature review

In addition, Extract 1.10 illustrates how the first part of such a title is often a 'teaser' (i.e., it stimulates interest in what is to come), while Extract 1.11 works a genre marker into the second part. Finally, you will have noticed that neither extract concludes with a full stop; that is true for most English titles, and indeed for headings at every level.

In some split titles, the first part may take the form of a question, as in the next two extracts.

TWO-PART TITLES BEGINNING WITH A QUESTION
Extract 1.12 [Scales 2022: 321]
Ever closer union? Unification, difference, and the 'Making of Europe', c. 950-c. 1350

Extract 1.13 [Harrison, Hole and Habibi 2020: 672]
Are you in or are you out? The importance of group saliency in own-group biases in face recognition

Alternatively, if seemingly less often, the question may come in the second part, as in Extract 1.14.

---

5   The question of whether or not to capitalise the first letter after the colon is a moot one. As these extracts show, both versions are acceptable.

TWO-PART TITLE ENDING WITH A QUESTION
Extract 1.14 [Shaw & Bailey 2009: 413]
Discourse analysis: what is it and why is it relevant to family practice?

Still other titles consist of noun phrases. This is probably the variant most likely to occur to speakers of many continental European languages, which are generally much 'nounier' than English. For that same reason it is to be used with discretion, as it is in Extracts 1.15 and 1.16.

NOUN-PHRASE TITLES
Extract 1.15 [Taylor 2020: 171]
Social categories in context

Extract 1.16 [Barnes 2020: 1]
Information management research and practice in the post-COVID-19 world

Also worth noting in the latter is the readiness of English to use multipart compound nouns (e.g., *information management research*) without any hyphens or intervening prepositions. Such compounds constitute one means of avoiding long strings of nouns connected only by prepositions, above all *of* (for some other means, see 3.4.1).

Often, the *–ing* form of a verb (in such cases technically a gerund) is used instead of a noun to inject a greater sense of dynamism into titles, as in these two examples.

TITLES STARTING WITH *-ING* FORMS
Extract 1.17 [Shipp 2021: 332]
Appointing a poet laureate: National and poetic identities in 1813

Extract 1.18 [Collier & Cox 2021: 275]
Governing urban resilience: Insurance and the problematization of climate change

In Extract 1.17, for example, *appointing* definitely sounds more dynamic (and less clumsy) than *the appointment of* would have done, and the same applies to *governing* as opposed to *the government of* in the second example.

Introductions

The other essential element of scene-setting is indeed a distinct introduction, often contained in a section with that heading. It serves several important purposes. Swales groups them into three so-called *moves* (Swales 1990; Swales & Feak 2012: 331).

> Move 1 – Establishing a research territory
> Move 2 – Establishing a niche
> Move 3 – Occupying the niche

In Move 1, you show why the research area is important and review the relevant literature; in Move 2 you identify the research gap you intend to fill; and in Move 3 you explain how you intend to fill it. The moves need to be clearly identifiable, with each consisting of at least one paragraph, though possibly more. Nevertheless, the introduction must remain just that: a section that merely prepares the ground for the rest of the story rather than telling the story itself. Its purpose, as Pollock (2021: 51) explains, is to "hook" the reader "so that their answer to the question 'Who cares?' is 'I do!'"

This 'so-what' question really is essential, yet often overlooked. Sometimes, the only enticement the authors offer is the mere existence of a research gap. The problem is that this gap may exist because it lacks any great interest. So what you really need to do is to build a strong case for filling it. Extract 1.19 is an example of how to build such a case by means of a (very cautious) "mini-critique" (Swales & Feak 2012: 348) of existing research.

> **JUSTIFICATION FOR FILLING A RESEARCH GAP**
> **Extract 1.19** [Islam & Sanderson 2022: 4-5][6]
> Within this small but feisty subfield of critical psychology, **critical voices within work and organizational psychology have been even more infrequent** (cf., Bal et al., 2019; Manroop, 2017; Mumby, 2019; Parker, 2009; Symon & Cassell, 2006; Weber, Höge, & Hornung, 2020). **This is surprising, given the location of worker experience at the heart of the labor process** (Braverman, 1974), and thus **at the**

---

6   *W-O = work and organizational*

crux of key social tensions – work and home life (Hatton, 2017), capital and labor (Burawoy, 1979), autonomy and control (Axel, 2009), recognition and redistribution (Fraser & Honneth, 2003). **Recognizing this deficit, calls have appeared to develop critical perspectives** in W-O psychology further (Bal et al., 2019), with conference meetings, journal special issues, and similar initiatives emerging within the field. These initiatives have not set out to form an autonomous subgroup or critical niche, but to build on experiences of work psychologists across the field in transversal, inclusive formats.

In other cases, existing research is portrayed in a positive light and the 'mini-critique' is aimed merely at a failure to follow it up. The 'gap' is thus essentially a missed opportunity. Extract 1.20 shows this technique in action.

JUSTIFICATION OF RESEARCH AS BUILDING ON EXISTING WORK
Extract 1.20 [Best & Hindmarsh 2019: 249]
This article aims to advance this third strand of work by attempting to elaborate our understanding of the ways in which people inhabit and constitute the sense and significance of space. [...] **While** there is a significant tradition of studies that take seriously the lived experience and social production of space, **we will show how** the adoption of an explicit interactional analytic lens can produce novel insights into the ways in which organizational members use, inhabit, experience and, in doing so, constitute their workspace.

Note how the authors of this example manage to combine respect for others' research with a modest, albeit very clear statement of why their own project adds something valuable to the field. The sentence starting with *while* sees to that.

There are no hard-and-fast rules about which details you should give away in the introduction and which you can save for later. It partly depends on how the rest of the paper is organised. If there is a separate section headed *Literature Review*, for example, then the introduction needs only a fairly cursory survey of existing research. Similarly, you may use the introduction to briefly outline your research design, while leaving the specifics for the Methods section.

One thing that should definitely be done at the 'scene-setting' stage is to define key terms, particularly if these are ambiguous and/or contested.

Should that be the case, you need to state clearly how you yourself are going to use them. Equally important is a (brief) critical review of how such terminology is used in the existing literature. The two aspects are addressed neatly in this example.

INTRODUCING CONTESTED TERMINOLOGY
Extract 1.21 [Brigstocke et al. 2021: 1359][7]
What, then, *is* authority? **In contrast to dominant geographical definitions of authority** that equate it with institutionalized command, sovereignty or legitimate power, **we propose** a more limited and specific definition of authority as a relation of guidance that takes place between free actors and is performatively enacted by recognizing inequalities in access to truth, experience or objectivity.

A further important point about the introduction – and one reason it is the last thing you will finalise – is that it should combine with the paper's conclusion to bookend what lies between them (a point we will return to in 1.2.4). This principle implies that each of these two sections should be noticeably shorter than the central parts of the paper. A disproportionately long introduction indicates that it is trying to do too much, and that parts of it need to be moved to later sections of the paper. (An overly long conclusion, on the other hand, is a sign of too much unfinished business.)

Introductions usually end with a so-called orientation paragraph, telling the reader what to expect. Extract 1.22 is a fairly typical example.

ORIENTATION PARAGRAPH AT THE END OF AN INTRODUCTION
Extract 1.22 [Llewellyn & Whittle 2019: 836]
The article is organized as follows. **In the first section**, **we review** the literature on lying, focusing in particular on the study of deceit in business and workplace settings. **Next, we outline** the ethnomethodological approach we take and the distinct methodological approach this involves. **We then analyse** one false claim from each setting. **The discussion draws together the findings** to present an ethnomethodological account of 'lying' in interaction. **The conclusion**

---

7   In the rest of the paragraph, not quoted here for reasons of space, the authors define five key terms that appear in their definition of 'authority': *guidance, actor, free, performatively enacted* and *recognition*.

broadens the discussion to consider the implications of our findings for developing our understanding of how 'cultures of deceit' perpetuate in the light of the defeasibility of lies.

The story is thus mapped out at the beginning – another difference between research stories and most fictional ones.

Conceptual background

Any research article will require some form of conceptual underpinning since readers will be keen to know what foundations your work rests on. This underpinning may come in various guises, depending on the discipline and type of paper. In theoretical ones, where it is itself the main focus of inquiry, it will most likely form part of the story's middle rather than its beginning. In empirical papers, on the other hand, it may appear in the introduction itself or in some other element of the scene-setting.

Theory – either an existing one or one of your own devising – is essential, because it supplies the interpretive framework required to make sense of the data in front of you. As Pollock (2021) puts it:

> Theory provides a story about the connections between phenomena, and why actions, events, structures, thoughts or feelings occur. It emphasizes the nature, direction, context and timing of relationships, and delves into underlying processes to understand the systematic reasons things occur or do not occur (p. 65).

Approaches to theory differ widely between disciplines, and not all disciplines require in-depth debates about it in every publication. Some fields, especially newer ones, may still be struggling to establish their theoretical credentials and therefore require all authors to make an explicit contribution to theory development. Others already have a well-established, largely uncontested and widely shared theoretical basis – and so need to invoke it only on the rare occasions that it is being challenged.

If a piece of research is based on hypotheses, then the theory section is where these are usually spelled out (and the section is sometimes named *Theory and Hypotheses*). Hypotheses make sense if a project explores the relationship between an independent variable (a cause) and a dependent variable (an effect). Clearly that does not always apply. Theoretical papers are not hypothesis-driven; nor are qualitative studies of complex social settings, or analyses of literary works, to name just a few examples.

The research question(s)

Swales' third move, 'occupying the niche', is about filling the research gap you have identified. That is where the research question (RQ) or questions come(s) in. Every project can – and indeed must – have at least one, even papers that are not hypothesis-driven. RQs are needed in both theoretical and applied research, and for qualitative as well as quantitative approaches.

An RQ is a question specifying what you are trying to find out or which specific problem you intend to tackle. In this it differs from 'the topic', which is much broader – usually too broad, in fact, to be translated into concrete research activity. If you're a student approaching a potential supervisor about a thesis, you will probably first talk to them about the kinds of *topic* you (and they) are interested in. But as soon as they give you the go-ahead to explore these further, you should start narrowing the topic down and distil an RQ from it.

So what makes a good research question? Again, it is difficult to generalise. But the following advice from a university writing centre should be serviceable across disciplines.

> A research question is the question around which you center your research. It should be:
>
> - **clear**: it provides enough specifics that one's audience can easily understand its purpose without needing additional explanation.
> - **focused**: it is narrow enough that it can be answered thoroughly in the space the writing task allows.
> - **concise**: it is expressed in the fewest possible words.
> - **complex**: it is not answerable with a simple "yes" or "no", but rather requires synthesis and analysis of ideas and sources prior to composition of an answer.
> - **arguable**: its potential answers are open to debate rather than accepted facts.[8]

An RQ with these qualities will give the reader a good idea of where you're headed, and it will help you assemble the theoretical and methodological toolkit that you need to get the research process under way. The following is an excellent example.

---

8   https://writingcenter.gmu.edu/writing-resources/research-based-writing/how-to-write-a-research-question; accessed 31 July 2022 (boldface and capitalisation as in original)

WELL FORMULATED RESEARCH QUESTION

Extract 1.23 [Guntermann & Beauvais 2022: 374]

This leaves us with an important unanswered question: Is the LGB vote uniform across groups within the queer community, with lesbian, gay and bisexual voters sharing similar political attitudes? Or do notable political differences exist within the LGB community?

Quite *where* the research question is placed is another thing that varies a good deal. In some cases, it may even appear in the article title or in the first lines of the story's beginning. More commonly, it will be delayed until the end of the introduction section or perhaps even longer, until the conclusion of the conceptual background or a literature review. But where it is actually revealed is not so relevant. What signals that the story's beginning has finished is a move away from the RQ's broad research context and towards actually tackling it.

In Brief
THE RESEARCH STORY'S BEGINNING

- The beginning part of an article sets the scene for what follows.
- It includes all the elements of the article that are necessary to set the scene: certainly the title and introduction, but perhaps also the conceptual background and/or a literature review.
- It locates the article in a broader research context.
- It justifies and sets out the research question(s) the paper will address, as well as any hypotheses.

1.2.3 The middle: Developing the plot

In our metaphorical terms, the middle is where the story's tempo quickens and the plot thickens. Precisely how that happens in research texts can vary widely. Even more so than with the beginning and the ending, it is difficult to specify how the relevant sections of the paper will be named, since not only disciplines and publication types are to be considered but also the specific topic. Only one generalisation can be made with confidence. The middle is where the scope of the story narrows, from the broad, outward-looking approach of the beginning to an unwavering focus on answering the

RQ. This narrowing is well illustrated in the hour-glass diagrams associated specifically with the AIMRaD structure (e.g., Cargill & O'Connor 2021: 14), but whose validity extends well beyond that approach.

Methods

One thing almost certain to be found in the research story's middle is a discussion of the methods used. (If the scene-setting did not include a conceptual background, then a section on theory is another likely element.) In AIMRaD structures, and in empirical papers generally, this discussion will come in a section explicitly headed *Methods* or *Data and Methods*. It describes what data were used, how they were sampled, collected and processed, and how they were analysed.

Importantly, you need to explain why you chose certain data but not others. Depending on your topic, that will mean answering a number of potential question such as these. Why did you choose articles from two tabloids but ignore quality papers? Why did you carry out interviews with adults between 30 and 50 but no other age groups? Why were the dramatist's early plays not included in the study? With good reason, Pollock (2021: 80) calls this explaining and justifying "the persuasive heart of your Methods section".

Another thing you will need to explain and justify is your choice of method. Again, the way you do so will be all the more convincing if you manage to anticipate and deflect your readers' criticism (Pollock 2021: 83). In fact, the most effective way of persuading readers that you have made the right choices is to explain step-by-step how you arrived at them. The Methods section thus itself becomes a story, in which, as Extract 1.24 illustrates, the 'narrator' can make an effective personal appearance.

> **JUSTIFYING THE CHOICE OF METHOD**
> **Extract 1.24** [Guess 2021: 1009-1010]
> Given the limitations of survey-based approaches to studying media exposure, **I follow the lead of pioneering scholars** who turned to third-party data on web visits to better understand online media consumption patterns (Gentzkow and Shapiro 2011; Tewksbury 2003). **Their work generated useful macrolevel evidence** by aggregating to the level of individual web domains.

To be of any use to the reader, the information provided in the Methods section needs to be very detailed. Generic statements – about having done 'textual analysis' or 'statistical analysis', for example – are not sufficient. Readers will want methods to be referred to in much more specific terms (e.g., as *corpus-assisted discourse studies* or *random-effects regression*); otherwise, they will not be able to judge whether the chosen methods were indeed appropriate. Nor would they be able to replicate the study if they so chose. (In practice, few people do, but creating the conditions under which they *might* is still considered the gold standard.)

While it is true that many articles do not include a specific Methods section, an explanation of how the writer approached their central research question will still have to appear somewhere. For instance, in the paper which forms the basis of Table 1.1 (in 1.1.2 above), the section headed *Places of joy: heritage after lockdown* is actually devoted to the sources of data and the methods used to analyse it, as explained in the preceding Introduction.

Results and findings

At last, the results. Again, the type of paper, the research design and the discipline will have an influence on whether there is a section headed *Results* or *Findings*. In quantitative empirical research, tables and charts are an obvious way of doing that. But no matter how they are presented, such elements must never be assumed to speak for themselves; what they show must also be described verbally (see 2.2.2). If your paper was driven by hypotheses, then the description of your results should restate them and indicate whether the results support them or not.

Qualitative findings, by contrast, can only be reported narratively (though the gist may be summarised in a table). To allow readers to judge whether your analyses are plausible, you need to share your textual evidence. This is why in qualitative papers the section(s) devoted to findings include numerous quotations from the texts under investigation. Yet, however vivid and to the point, these do not speak for themselves; like numerical results, data extracts must be commented on in the running text.

In Brief
THE RESEARCH STORY'S MIDDLE

- The middle part of an article focuses solely on answering the research question(s).
- It may do that in a wide variety of ways, but it will certainly contain information on the following (unless for some reason they were dealt with in the lead-up to the research question(s):
  - □ the data and methods used
  - □ the conceptual background
  - □ the results and findings

1.2.4 The ending: Rounding it all off

And so the research story draws to its close. What demarcates its ending is a return to the broader perspective of the beginning. In other words, the results described in the middle part of the article are related to the conceptual background and/or to the conversations in the field as whole. Extract 1.25 makes this connection explicit.

'RE-BROADENING' OF FOCUS AT THE START OF A STORY'S ENDING
Extract 1.25 [Wight & Cooper 2022: 7]
It is with this in mind that we return to the question posed at the start of this paper and argue that binge-watching and the shift to surveillance capitalism poses challenges for teaching the kinds of critical understanding about representation that underpins Cultural Studies. For instance, the way streaming companies draw upon the liberatory energy of the 'popular' resembles and differs from the work of Cultural Studies in significant ways.

As part of this re-broadening, you may also want to address your findings' practical applications, as well as the impact of your research outside academia, in social domains such as politics or business. The AIMRaD template includes a standard heading, *Discussion*, under which these things can be done, but once again that is far from universal. In narrative terms, the action is brought to a climax of some sort and a denouement, literally the 'untying' of Aristotle's knot: that is, the resolution of the problem or conundrum posed at the outset (Pollock 2021: 15).

Discussion

The exact division of labour between discussion and conclusion (however these may be headed) is yet again hard to pinpoint. The first of them will typically include an interpretation of your findings in the light of the conceptual framework. Often, it will also talk about the paper's limitations (in a subsection which may or may not be flagged up as such), although these are sometimes postponed until the very end of the article. Every paper, however good, is bound to have flaws, and it is advisable to confess these openly rather than wait for others to point them out: questions that were left unasked; questions that the chosen method could not answer; or explanations that could not be made fully watertight because the data used was either insufficient or of the wrong kind. Being open about such problems is no guarantee that reviewers and other readers will accept your justification. But if they do, they will appreciate that the limitations of one project often provide the seeds of the next one.

Extract 1.26 exemplifies such pre-emptive confessions well. The part of the paragraph shown here includes two of them (and in the part not shown here a further two are mentioned at similar length).

ACKNOWLEDGING LIMITATIONS

Extract 1.26 [Winchenbach, Hanna & Miller 2022: 804]

This study **has several limitations**. The **focus on men ignores the important role that women play** in fisheries, which is increasingly recognised in the literature (see for example Kleiber et al., 2015). Omitting the voices of women was not deliberate but determined by those who chose to participate in the research. Additionally, **we omit an in-depth engagement with community-level dimensions** of coastal and marine tourism diversification. As such, researching the experiences of women and other key stakeholders, as well as partici-pants' interrelationship with actants in tourism diversification would arguably lead to more nuanced and varied understandings of identity.

It is worth noting how the first *mea culpa* (i.e., the ignoring of women's role) is followed by an explanation, with no attempt made to turn it into an excuse (*determined by those who chose to participate*). Following the second (i.e., the omission of local engagement), the authors use another common strategy: reframing the two issues as an opportunity for follow-up research.

Conclusion

An article's conclusion is typically a mixture of various things: part summary, part outlook, part impact, part further research. It also provides the opportunity to bookend your story by connecting explicitly back to the beginning. This technique, well-illustrated in the example below, is very common, and certainly very effective.

> **CONCLUSION LINKING BACK TO THE INTRODUCTION**
> **Extract 1.27** [Monteiro & Adler 2022: 449]
> **Let us conclude by returning to the puzzle motivating this paper** – the discrepancy between the declining scholarly interest in bureaucracy and the persistence of bureaucracy as the predominant form of organization.

And then, at long last, you will get to the point of writing the very last paragraph. As far as best practices for paragraph writing are concerned, the closing paragraph must clearly fulfil the same requirements as all the others (see Chapter 2). Yet, over and above that, it carries a heavier rhetorical burden. This is why everything we will discuss in future chapters – about designing effective paragraphs and constructing sentences with reader appeal, among other things – is particularly relevant for that final clincher. A strong ending will convince the reader that the time spent listening to your research story was not wasted.

In Brief
THE RESEARCH STORY'S ENDING

- The ending of an article returns to the broad research context examined in the beginning.
- It discusses the results and findings in that context, and draws conclusions.
- It usually also 'confesses' any limitations the article may have, such as restrictions due to the data, method, or perspective adopted.

1.3 Text appeal

Up to this point, we have talked about the technical aspects of planning texts: about dividing them up into visibly distinct sections and subsections, and imagining them as a form of story with a beginning, middle and ending. That in itself makes the text more easily readable because it helps readers to find their way around it, either on a straight route from beginning to end or by jumping directly to parts of particular interest to them. But it also inevitably introduces an element of uniformity that doesn't necessarily promote pleasurable reading.

Writers can break down this uniformity by deliberately introducing elements of variety. That is a theme we will return to repeatedly throughout the book. In particular, it will feature in the closing sections of the next two chapters, where we will consider ways of making paragraphs and sentences more varied. But we will begin here by looking at ways of lending the research text as a whole a degree of variety.

The first way to do that is to avoid starting a number of successive paragraphs – the smallest units apparent to the reader at a glance – with the same grammatical pattern. Examples of beginnings that can all too easily become repetitive are *the* followed by a noun, or an adverb like *interestingly* followed by a comma. A best practice example is provided by Extract 1.28, which shows the opening phrases of ten successive paragraphs making up a subsection entitled *Non-state actor support of sustainability and climate initiatives.*

VARIATION IN PARAGRAPH OPENINGS
Extract 1.28 [Coen, Hermann & Pegram 2022: 3-4][9]
The involvement of the corporate sector in ...
Reflecting deeper critiques of ...
During the formative years of ...
As noted in the introduction, ...
For instance, the GRI ...
Beyond the broader ESG-focused CCIs discussed above, ...
However, in an important study which ...
Another significant non-state actor which ...

---

9   *GRI = Global Reporting Initiative; ESG = Environmental, Social and Governance; CCIs = Corporate Climate Initiatives.*

Finally, reflecting growing efforts to ...
Based on the remit of these CCIs, ...

Significantly, none of the paragraphs in question is particularly complex or at all lengthy (other than the last, which consists of four sentences, none contains more than 3). That undoubtedly helps make the variety of paragraph beginnings apparent to the reader.

In this regard, a further consideration is paragraph length. Of course, paragraphs in general should not be too long (see 2.1). What we are driving at here is the powerful effect of making the occasional one genuinely short (three or four sentences, say), especially if it comes at the beginning or end of a headed subdivision. This brings us to paragraph*ing*: the act of dividing a text up into paragraphs, and specifically of dividing an existing paragraph into two or more shorter ones.

The challenge in doing this is to identify points at which a particular paragraph can be divided. The most obvious signal that a division is feasible would be that the paragraph has moved away from the 'single main idea' which it set out to deal with (see 2.1), or has perhaps moved on to an aspect of that topic distinct enough to justify paragraph status. Another signal would be the introduction of a different perspective. Outwardly, shifts of this sort are typically made apparent by linkers like *however, nevertheless, by contrast* or *on the other hand*, or by expressions such as *according to other writers* or *in our view*. You don't have to act on these signals, of course. But if you do decide to take action, then you will need to ensure that the new paragraph you create, like the existing one, has the essential features of an English paragraph. And these are what we will be talking about in the next chapter.

Chapter 1: The takeaways

- Research writing involves creative expression within constraints.
- The principal constraint consists in the conventions applying to particular types of research genres.
- A further constraint is the requirement to organise research texts systematically, with the organisation often taking the form of a hierarchy.
- The hierarchy is made apparent to readers through the appropriate choice of (numbered) headings.
- Research texts, in particular journal articles, can be pictured as 'research stories', an image that highlights:
  - □ the need for them to progress towards some sort of climax
  - □ their three-part structure
- The abstract stands outside this structure but is a vital part of the article, and so is to be written with just as much care as the paper itself.
- The first part of the 'story', its beginning, is where the scene is set.
  - □ It places the text in the broader research context.
  - □ It leads up to a research question or questions (RQs).
  - □ It therefore includes the title, the introduction, and perhaps also other sections.
- The story's middle develops the plot. It focuses on answering the RQs, and generally contains sections on data and methods, and on results and findings.
- The ending is where the story is rounded off.
  - □ It returns to the broader perspective adopted in the beginning.
  - □ It answers the RQ(s) by discussing the results/findings.
  - □ It draws conclusions.
  - □ It usually 'confesses' the study's limitations.
- Over and above these formal requirements, you need to make your research article appealing to its readers by:
  - □ varying paragraph openings
  - □ ensuring that at least some paragraphs are genuinely short

2 *One step at a time*: Designing paragraphs

> *Having imagination, it takes you an hour to write a paragraph that, if you were unimaginative, would take you only a minute.*
> FRANKLIN P. ADAMS (1881 – 1960)[1]

The second pillar on which a good research article rests consists in the quality of the paragraphs that make up each of its (sub)sections. That may not sound like a big deal, but it is. For, although the notion of a paragraph exists in many languages, it seems particularly delineated in English. Designing paragraphs in line with the expectations of English readers of academic texts is thus no easy matter, even for native speakers. Yet without the skills required, the chances of writing an effective research article are minimal.

In order to acquire those skills, it is necessary to understand how English paragraphs 'work'. Like whole research texts, they have three distinct parts: a beginning, a middle and an end. The crucial point is that each of these parts has a specific function. The beginning is where the writer sets the scene, establishing what the paragraph will discuss (and, by implication, what it won't) and, most likely, drops some hints as to how it will go about the discussion. Next, in the middle, the paragraph's topic is developed in some way. How that is done will depend heavily on the section where the paragraph is located and the topic itself, so that we can make only rather general comments. And last, but very definitely not least, the paragraph's end is its denouement, a resolution of the preceding discussion.

---

1   Commas added.

2.1 The essence of English paragraphs

So what's special about English paragraphs? First of all, as we mentioned in the previous chapter, they are units of meaning, each of which develops a single main idea (or perhaps a well-defined aspect of an idea). To put that differently, a paragraph is a single step in the argument of the (sub)section to which it belongs. In developing its main idea, it drives the argument forward to the next step in line with certain principles.

Principles

Readers of English texts – specifically academic texts – have certain expectations about the way a paragraph is designed internally, expectations raised by well-established conventions. If communication is to be easy and effective, those expectations must be met. So, even if writers may occasionally depart from the conventions when they have good reason, generally they will respect them. Essentially there are six of these principles, as follows.

1. A paragraph **begins with a topic sentence**, the purpose of which is to set out the main idea, or aspect of an idea, that the paragraph will develop. Everything in the rest of the paragraph will relate in one way or another to that idea.
2. The topic sentence is **followed by one or more supporting sentences** of various types. Among other things, they may describe subcategories of the main idea, provide some examples of it or develop a line of logical reasoning leading up to it or based on it.
3. The **final sentence** of a paragraph generally represents some sort of **resolution**. It may act as a climax to the preceding items: for example,

by giving the clinching explanation for a particular development (e.g., *above all, X is the result of ...; the fundamental cause, however, is ...*). It may echo the topic sentence in order to drive home the main idea. On other occasions, it may (also) serve as a transition to the next paragraph. Admittedly, the final sentence is sometimes simply a further supporting sentence, but then the support it offers should be especially strong.

4. As can be deduced from the above, paragraphs in academic texts consist of **at least three sentences**. However, this three-sentence rule is really a lower limit; good paragraphs usually consist of somewhere between four and eight sentences. There are also exceptions to the rule (which we will come back to later). Nevertheless, novice writers are well advised to begin by mastering the default structure before seeking to depart from it.

5. Either directly or indirectly, **all the sentences are connected** to each other and to the main idea. The connections between them may be established implicitly, by their content. Or they may be made explicit, by various cohesive devices (to be discussed in Chapter 5).

6. The **start** of a new paragraph is indicated by **indenting its first line**. In other words, its first line begins a little to the right of the standard left margin. (Less usually, the same effect is achieved by a blank line, though never by both.) In British English, the variety used in this book,[2] paragraphs immediately below a headline begin flush left; in American English, they may also be indented.

In Brief
THE ENGLISH PARAGRAPH

- A paragraph begins with a topic sentence.
- It continues with various supporting sentences.
- It generally ends with a concluding sentence.
- It almost always consists of at least three sentences.
- Its sentences are connected to each other and to the paragraph's topic.
- Its start is generally indicated by indenting.

---

2   Except in illustrative extracts originally written in other varieties.

Length

The fourth of our basic principles stipulates a minimum paragraph length, but what about the upper limit? That is a question hard to answer since a 'single main idea' is a fuzzy concept. On the one hand, that gives writers some flexibility when it comes to paragraphing (see 1.3) but, on the other, that same fuzziness makes it hard to decide how far an idea can be stretched.

Obviously, if you feel that you have really moved on to a new idea which you have a substantial amount to say about, then it is probably time to start a new paragraph. Another factor is the degree of emphasis you wish to accord an idea, a point we will take up in Section 7.2.2. And, thirdly, there is the question of how much you can expect the average reader to take in before they need to pause and review what they have just read. As a very broad rule of thumb, if you note during editing that a standard A4 page with 1.5 line spacing contains only one paragraph break, then it is certainly worth thinking about introducing some more.

To draw a comparison with eating, a paragraph ought to be a bite-sized chunk: big enough to give you something to chew on, but small enough to digest in one go. The 'three-sentence rule' is intended to ensure that the first condition is met. As for meeting the second condition, that is for you to decide, based on your own experience and careful observation of good practice.

Extract 2.1 is a fairly typical example of an academic paragraph structured and written in line with these principles.

A TYPICAL WELL-STRUCTURED PARAGRAPH

Extract 2.1 [Caserta & Madsen 2019: 9-10]

Another interesting potential consequence of these developments is their impact on the national differentiation of legal practice. Today, a law degree from a national university is needed to practice law, e.g., in England. Online technology, however, is not geographically attached in the same way and, at least for the simpler tasks, the legal work involved with providing on-line legal services can easily be done from low-cost countries. Similarly, since on-line services work best in delineated legal areas so far, it is possible to train cheaper service providers – new forms of tech paralegals – to oversee the computer-driven conflict resolution and legal advice. Again, for lawyers currently making a living out of dealing with less complicated legal cases, this will pose serious challenges to their future business.

The initial sentence indicates clearly the paragraph's topic and introduces the key terms *national, differentiation* and *legal practice* (as well as creating a connection to the previous paragraph by means of *another*: see 5.3). The second sentence describes the current situation, which is then contrasted with two developments in the online world that are undermining it. In the final sentence, a conclusion is drawn that is related back to the topic sentence (*legal cases* → *legal practice*).

The hamburger structure

As the above example shows, the six basic principles have important implications for paragraph structure that are often discussed in metaphorical terms under the heading of the hamburger structure. This repeats the points underlying the notion of 'bite-sized chunks' introduced earlier (a hamburger needs to be ample but not too big to bite into) while also highlighting the internal make-up of the paragraph.

In the hamburger metaphor, the first and last sentences of the paragraph are represented by the top and bottom halves of the burger bun, with the supporting sentence(s) being the 'meat' of the argument ('meat' in the sense of 'main and most important part'). Of course, like any metaphor, this image has its weaknesses. For instance, since the topic sentence comes at the top of the paragraph, it corresponds to the top half of the bun – and no actual hamburger is assembled from the top down. Equally, as we have seen, the final sentence might actually be a further layer of 'meat', in which case the reader would be left covered in metaphorical grease.

Yet the image has long been firmly established in the US, by far the world's largest research 'market', and for good reason. First, it reminds us that the way a paragraph is assembled is just as important as its content, or even more so. To make something that will pass as a 'hamburger', it is not enough to bring together the ingredients (bun, patty, lettuce and tomato, plus the tasty extras), however good they may be, and slap them down unthinkingly on a plate. They need to be arranged in the way people expect a hamburger to be arranged. Similarly, in writing, for several sentences to form a proper paragraph they must be arranged in the right order and bound together, as the patty is to the bun. If they are jumbled up and/or unconnected, their propositional value (i.e., what each one expresses) may remain the same, but they will not form a meaningful whole that actually makes a point. It is not sentences but paragraphs that really provide food for thought.

Second, the hamburger image is a reminder of the 'minimum three sentences' principle. Just occasionally, it is true, a paragraph may consist of only two sentences. (One-sentence paragraphs really ought to be avoided in academic writing, though not in, say, journalism.) A two-sentence paragraph is permissible when its sole function is to serve as an introduction: to a bulleted list, to a series of full paragraphs (which may be numbered or opened by *first, second, third* etc.) or to two or more subsections. Thus the two sentences in Extract 2.2 are followed by two subsections with their own headings, while those that make up Extract 2.3 are followed by a list of five bullet points.

VALID EXCEPTIONS FROM THE THREE-SENTENCE RULE
Extract 2.2 [Gastil & Sprain 2011: 149]
How one should act in a group depends on one's context because the broad concept of a "small group" contains a tremendous variety of group types. Before exploring those variations, the first task is tracing the boundaries of the small group category.[2]

Extract 2.3 [Guess 2021: 1012]
Given the amount of researcher discretion involved at each stage, I apply different combinations of preprocessing and analytic steps to the data and report the results of each, either in the article or the Supporting Information. The primary decisions are as follows: [...]

However, although such pairs of sentences are set off from the rest of the text, they are perhaps best not considered 'paragraphs' at all, at least not in the full sense of the word. Rather than making a point in their own right, such paragraphs merely prepare readers for what is coming next. They are, in fact, elaborate 'advance organisers' (see 5.2.4 and 5.3). Legitimate, and indeed necessary, as such passages may be at certain junctures in the text, they are certainly not models for what a standard paragraph ought to look like. For that, best stick to the three-sentence rule.

With regard to maximum paragraph length, the hamburger metaphor reflects our earlier food-related image of the 'bite-sized chunk'. Not that we are suggesting it is a good idea to eat a whole hamburger in one go. But if the patty is too thick (i.e., if the paragraph contains too many sentences), the burger becomes extremely hard to eat, and its appearance may take the edge off the appetite of all but the very hungriest.

2.2 The components of a paragraph

Now, having discussed the implications of the hamburger structure, we will look more closely at the three layers of which it consists. As you may be relieved to hear, that means abandoning food-related metaphors and, rather than layers, we will talk of a paragraph's *components*. We will begin with the topic sentence before proceeding to the body, or middle part, and to the final sentence.

2.2.1 The topic sentence

As we mentioned earlier, a paragraph's topic sentence is where the 'main idea' is introduced. However, a topic sentence may also be viewed as a rudimentary map to guide readers on their journey through the paragraph it opens. At the very least, it will inform them of their destination, the point which the paragraph as a whole will lead up to. But, as well as that, it will often point to some of the key features they will encounter on the way – people, events, abstract concepts – and the order in which these will be met: in other words, how the paragraph will be developed.

In performing this function, topic sentences typically include keywords and key concepts that re-occur several times in the paragraph, forming a web of semantic relationships that hold it together and enable readers to make sense of it without too much effort.

> **KEYWORDS IN A TOPIC SENTENCE**
> **Extract 2.4** [Sytch & Kim 2021: 181]
> For social **identification** effects to operate, people do not need to know each other personally. Social **identification** can emanate from an asynchronous social affiliation between actors, such as attending the same educational institution at different times. Although an inter-personal relationship can boost the level of social **identification**, the primary factor that triggers social **identification** is actors' belonging to the same social category. In other words, people can claim common **identification** through their shared institutional membership even when personal connections are absent.

Extract 2.4 illustrates these principles in action. Its topic sentence includes four words that are either repeated later in the paragraph, or are echoed by close synonyms: *social, identification, personally* and *people.*

It's worth bearing in mind that topic sentences are what skim readers will focus on to get a rather more detailed overview of the text than they can glean just from headings. So to make life easy for them, and thus encourage them to read the text in full, writers can try to ensure that their topic sentences make a reasonably coherent chain. Indeed, a useful editing tip is to read the topic sentences of the paragraphs making up a (sub)section as if they were a single text to see whether it makes a decent summary of the part concerned.

Apart from those relating to content, which we have just discussed, there are no rules for what topic sentences should look like. Arguably, relatively short ones are likely to be most effective; and if not short, they should at least have a simple, transparent structure. Extracts 2.5 to 2.7 are good examples. (As a topic sentence's effectiveness can only be judged in relation to what follows, the quoted extracts also include one or two additional sentences.)

EFFECTIVE TOPIC SENTENCES

Extract 2.5 [Spence 2021: 2]

In the digital economy, the existence of more than one mega-platform is a sign of market health. However, the mega-platforms must sufficiently overlap. Both the US and China have a handful of mega-platforms; [...]

Extract 2.6 [Sanscartier 2020: 51]

Episteme corresponds to scientific knowledge. For Flyvbjerg (2001, p. 56), the key characteristic of episteme is that such knowledge exists independently of context, such as the universal laws of physics. They may then be applied to specific contexts to calculate, for example, the trajectory of an astronomical object. [...]

Extract 2.7 [Moore et al. 2017: 4]

Do researchers recognize excellence when they see it? The short answer is no. This can be seen most easily when different potential measures of "excellence" conflict in their assessment of a single paper, project, or individual. [...]

Extract 2.7 is particularly noteworthy because the topic sentence is phrased as a question – an interesting device not uncommon in English, but much less so in other academic writing cultures such as German.

In all our examples so far, the topic sentence was positioned right at the start of the paragraph. Yet, as the following two examples show, that need not always be the case (although it must certainly be very near to the start). In Extract 2.8, it functions perfectly well despite coming second since it is so closely related to the first; indeed, were *therefore* replaced with *so*, the two could be written as a single sentence without any change in meaning.

> **ATYPICAL BUT EFFECTIVE TOPIC SENTENCES**
> **Extract 2.8** [Jenkins & Delbridge 2020: 3]
> As Grover (2005, p. 155) observed, 'very little is straightforward about lying and honesty'. **Therefore, our first challenge in studying lying is to define it.** For Bok (1980, p. 13), lying involves the intention to mislead [...]. Lying is when we conceal the truth, act in a dishonest manner and provide false information with the intention to deceive.
>
> **Extract 2.9** [Dempsey 2019: 775]
> **The question is: does this matter? Do we need more diversity in authorship in order to see more diversity in the past? I argue that this is imperative.** Embracing different and diverse voices would enhance our understanding of both the past and the present. [...]

That even more extreme deviations from the standard can still work is illustrated by Extract 2.9. Here, all the first three sentences, the first two of which are questions, effectively combine to fulfil the topic sentence function. Of course, the two questions could be moved to the end of the preceding paragraph, but the result would be a certain loss of rhetorical effect. In other words, the issue of what makes a good topic sentence cannot be completely reduced to standard formulae. As ever, the way forward is through critical reading designed to pick up best practice.

So far, we have talked only about those functions of the topic sentence that point *forward* to the rest of the paragraph that it introduces. Yet the topic sentence is also important in pointing *back* to the paragraph that precedes it, and sometimes even further back. These semantic links between paragraphs may be weaker than those within them, but they are still significant; after all, the whole text needs to hang together, not just the sentences within each paragraph. We will return to this point in Section 5.3.

> **In Brief**
> **WHAT DOES A TOPIC SENTENCE DO?**
>
> - It sets out the main idea to which the paragraph is devoted.
> - It provides a 'map' of the paragraph, indicating the destination and perhaps the 'route' by which that will be reached.
> - It usually includes keywords that occur repeatedly in the paragraph.
> - It often points back to the preceding paragraph or even further.

2.2.2 The 'meaty' middle

Let us assume you have written a neat topic sentence which says what the paragraph is about. The challenge now is to provide support for that main idea by developing the argument. As for how to do that, it is difficult to generalise and presumptuous to give advice. After all, no book on academic writing can ever dictate *what* you are supposed to write!

There are only two areas where it does make sense to point out some general principles – with all due caution, of course, and in the spirit of offering assistance rather than as *ex cathedra* pronouncements. One, to be discussed in Chapter 5, is the signalling of connections between the paragraph's various points by a range of semantic and grammatical devices. The other area, which we will discuss in the following, relates to developing arguments consistently and in ways that readers can follow easily.

Even if there is no magic recipe that will guarantee that your arguments turn out perfectly every time, it is possible to identify certain features of successful English paragraphs. Specifically, these tend to share the following characteristics:

- The argument proceeds step by step and in a linear fashion.
- The steps conform to a widely recognised pattern.

Such patterns include: comparing objects, situations, concepts, and individuals or groups; giving examples of ideas or phenomena; narrating stories using forward chronology (i.e., 'earlier' before 'later'); moving from 'general' to 'specific' or vice-versa (but not a mixture of the two); and various combinations of these and others.

Our next two examples illustrate these patterns. Extract 2.10 is a typical chronological paragraph, held together by the various dates and other time references (*in the first half of the nineteenth century; as the built-up area continued to expand*). This extract also provides a good example of a final sentence that echoes a topic sentence (see 2.2.3).

CHRONOLOGICAL PARAGRAPH DEVELOPMENT

Extract 2.10 [Heblich, Redding & Sturm 2020: 2068-2069]

In the first half of the nineteenth century, there was no municipal authority for the entire built-up area of Greater London, and public goods were largely provided by local parishes and vestries (centered around churches). [...] In response to the growing public health challenges created by an expanding population, the MBW [Metropolitan Board of Works] was founded **in 1855**. [...] With the aim of creating a central municipal government with the powers required to deliver public services effectively, the LCC [London County Council] was formed **in 1889**. [...] As the built-up area continued to expand, the concept of Greater London emerged, which was ultimately reflected in the replacement of the LCC by the Greater London Council (GLC) **in 1965.** Following the abolition of the GLC **in 1985** by the government of Margaret Thatcher, Greater London again had no central municipal government, until the creation of the GLA **in 1999.**

The development displayed in the next example is rather more complex. It makes use both of comparison (*what differentiates; while*) and of exemplification (*for example; some common WM tasks*).

COMPLEX PARAGRAPH DEVELOPMENT

Extract 2.11 [Flaim & Blaisdell 2020: 1176-1177]

WM [working memory] describes the ability to hold a limited amount of information over the short term (seconds to minutes). **What differentiates** WM from STM [short-term memory] is that WM involves manipulating the stored information or engaging in a secondary task while the to-be-recalled information is held in memory (Baddeley, 2003; Conway et al., 2002). **For example**, STM might involve holding in memory a list of items until their recall is requested, **while** WM would involve performing mathematical operations, counting, or some other transformation while encoding a list of to be recalled items. **Some common WM tasks are** the complex span task, n-back task (Au et al., 2015; Shelton, Elliott, Matthews, Hill, & Gouvier, 2010), and reverse span task (Oberauer, Süß, Schulze, Wilhelm, & Wittmann, 2000).

Linearity

No matter how a paragraph is developed, the key is always linearity. Readers familiar with well-written English paragraphs do not appreciate them going round in circles. Readers expect the argument to follow the obvious order. Writers are supposed to move patiently from A to B, then B to C, and then C to D, and not to go straight from A to D before doubling back to B. It is true that paragraphs which violate the principle of linearity may still be interpretable. But they place a considerable extra burden on the reader, namely that of putting the jumbled elements back into the correct order. The problems of understanding which can be caused when writers abandon linearity are illustrated in Makeover 2.1, along with some means of addressing them.

In the *Before* paragraph, the reader is given the impression that, following an initial reference to the (disputed) reasons for high growth, the paragraph will focus on the effects. Yet, after a single sentence, the discussion returns to the causes. The writer has attempted to bridge the resultant gap using the idea of 'agreement'. However, that refers to an essentially secondary point and also undermines the more important contrast between causes (disputed) and effects (undisputed). It therefore confuses as much as it enlightens. The paragraph's last two sentences then remain on the subject of causes, providing further details about the point made, and apparently dismissed, at the start of the first supporting sentence. The result is a feeling that, rather than moving forward, the argument has gone round in a circle, along with uncertainty as to the paragraph's intended meaning.

In the *After* paragraph, by contrast, this last issue is resolved right at the outset by a more informative topic sentence. The three supporting sentences all relate to the topic announced there, the causes of growth. The concluding sentence, clearly distinguished by the contrastive linker *however*, then moves the argument forward to the issue of effects. Throughout, progress has been strictly linear, and the product is a paragraph that is easy to read and leaves no room for confusion.

MAKEOVER 2.1: MAINTAINING LINEARITY WITHIN A PARAGRAPH

Before

Over the last decade, the country has experienced consistently high annual growth rates. Whereas there is considerable debate about the reasons for these, the effects are not in dispute. They include both a sharp decline in unemployment and an improvement in living standards for most of the population. Most informed observers also agree that high growth derived from large injections of foreign capital, but they differ widely as to what attracted these. Were the institutional reforms of 2008 the key factor? Or was it the massive economic liberalisation that really made the difference?

[paragraph from the introduction of a fictional journal paper.]

After

Over the last decade, the country has experienced consistently high annual growth rates, the reasons for which are the subject of consider- able debate. Most informed observers agree that high growth derived from large injections of foreign capital, but they differ widely as to what attracted these. Were the institutional reforms of 2008 the key factor? Or was it massive economic liberalisation that really made the difference? However, there is no dispute about the boom's effects, which include both a sharp decline in unemployment and an improvement in living standards for most of the population.

That said, even the best writers will occasionally want to lay out their argument in a less orthodox way, perhaps by departing from the linearity principle. There is no law against this. If the departure takes up more than one or two sentences, however, the writer must let their readers know what they are doing, both where the departure begins and where it ends and linearity is resumed. Some means of doing that are indicated in Toolbox 2.1. In fact, these are clear examples of the reader guidance to be discussed in Section 7.1.

Toolbox 2.1 SIGNALLING DEPARTURES FROM LINEARITY	
Start of departure	**End of departure**
This decline had serious consequences, which we will return to shortly. First, though, let us say a brief word about its causes.	*Returning now to the consequences of the decline, ...*
Leaving aside the consequences of this decline for a moment, we will briefly examine its causes.	*Having considered the decline's causes, we return now to its effect.*
Before considering the effects of this decline, we should briefly remind ourselves of its causes.	*However, what really concerns us here are not causes but consequences, to which we now turn.*

Bullet points

Despite what we said at the outset of this section, there are two specific forms of paragraph development about which it is possible to give some guidance. The first relates to a logical structure that frequently underlies a paragraph or a part of one. That structure is a list, a list of categories, of reasons or outcomes, of examples – of whatever, in fact. Indicating such lists in the paragraph's running text can be problematic if the individual items are of any significant length. Even if they aren't, numbering them, either by *first, second, ...,* or by numbers or letters in brackets, may work well now and again, but becomes intrusively repetitive if done too often.

A possible way out of this dilemma is to make use of bullet points. It is true that these may smack of PowerPoint presentations and may be associated more with business than with academia. But – as long as your publisher or editor is happy with the idea – they can be highly effective in research papers, not least because they serve to highlight points as well as enumerate them. If you do decide to use them, then you should observe the standard linguistic principles set out in Toolbox 2.2.

Toolbox 2.2	
THE 'DOS AND DON'TS' OF BULLETED LISTS	
Do ...	**Don't ...**
■ Include only items that share a common feature.	■ Introduce disparate items (e.g., a don't in a list of dos).
■ Leave the list title unbulleted.	■ Make the title part of the list itself by bulleting it.
■ Keep items fairly short.	■ Include items that consist of more than one sentence.
■ Make items grammatically parallel.	■ Use a mixture of different grammatical structures (e.g., full sentences, noun phrases).

With regard to the last point in Toolbox 2.2, certain grammatical structures are associated with particular item types. Specifically, lists of aims or purposes are frequently expressed by infinitive forms, while for describing the means to these ends one typically uses the *–ing* forms of verbs. Thus, to take an example from university administration, a list of departmental goals might read something like: *to improve teaching quality*; *to increase research output*; *to raise public visibility*. And the list of measures designed to achieve these goals might be phrased along the following lines: *by providing greater opportunities for staff development*; *by advertising vacancies more widely*, and so on.

Tables and figures

It is also possible to make some general comments about bolstering an argument through the use of tables and figures of various sorts (graphs, diagrams and images). These can never stand alone; they, or at least their key points, must also be discussed in the running text. They are numbered in sequence, either continuously throughout the article or, if there are numbered sections, beginning anew in each one of them (so the last table in Section 3 will be labelled 'Table 3.4', say, and the first in Section 4 'Table 4.1'). Tables and figures are numbered separately (so that 'Table 2' may be followed by 'Figure 1'). In all other ways, they are treated identically.

Tables and figures must be separated from the running text and given a suitable title and number. The positioning – above or below the table or figure in question – will be laid down in publishers' guidelines. Extracts 2.12 and 2.13 provide good examples.

TYPICAL TABLE TITLES
Extract 2.12 [Howarth & Quaglia 2021: 1560; original emboldening]
Table 1. Growing divergence in the Eurozone (five largest national economies).

Extract 2.13 [Fleming 2021: 15; original emboldening]
Figure 2. Marginal Effect of Government Seat Share on the Size of Post-Election Reshuffles.
Horizontal lines indicate 90% confidence intervals.

Extract 2.13 illustrates how the titles of tables and figures can be followed, on this occasion on a new line, by explanatory information about the table or figure itself, often in a smaller font size.

Titles should be kept as short as is consistent with giving precise guidance about the content of the table or figure. Unless the one concerned is entirely the author's own work (e.g., a table reporting empirical results), the title must include source references (see Chapter 6). If only the base data were taken from elsewhere, and not the form in which they are now presented, that can be noted by a phrase such as *based on*.

Like their titles, the tables and figures themselves should contain as little non-relevant information as possible. For instance, if a graph is intended to compare Germany's economic performance specifically with Spain's, then it is neither sensible nor effective to merely reproduce a table giving details for all EU member states (even if those referring to the two countries are highlighted in some way). Instead, a fresh table is required.

Last but not least, special care should be taken with numbers and amounts of money taken from sources in languages other than English. The main points are summarised in Toolbox 2.3, and some are illustrated in the example that precedes it.

NUMBERS IN AN ENGLISH ACADEMIC TEXT
Extract 2.14 [Howarth & Quaglia 2021: 1565]
The provision of grants was reduced from €500bn – sought by the Commission, France, Germany and Southern European member states – to €390bn. Of this amount, only €312.5bn would form specific

support for pandemic-hit member states (the Recovery and Resilience Facility, RRF), while the remaining €77.5bn would top up existing EU programmes.

Toolbox 2.3[3] **WRITING NUMBERS AND SUMS OF MONEY**	
Numbers (fractional divisions)	1.35 ["one point three five"]
Numbers (thousands and above)	10,000 ["ten thousand"] 73,000,000; 73 million; 73m 4,000,000,000; 4 billion; 4bn
Sums of money (UK)	16 pounds / 16 dollars £16 / $16 GBP 16 / USD 16

2.2.3 The final sentence

In Section 2.1, we remarked that a paragraph's final sentence can form part of the development that takes place in the middle section. Yet even where that is the case, it will generally represent a culmination of sorts: the most important or interesting cause, consequence or example of a phenomenon, or the endpoint of a process, for instance. To meet this expectation, you can raise the profile of the final sentence in various ways, for instance:

- By a linker such as *above all, last but not least* or *what is more*;
- By an adjective in the superlative form (e.g., *the most important consequence; the most striking example*);
- By a cleft-sentence structure (see Section 7.2.2), such as *what gives particular emphasis to a sentence is …*

However you do this, it is especially important that the final sentence observes the principle of end focus (see 3.2.2).

Where the final sentence is a genuine concluding sentence (i.e., not merely a further form of development), it will typically echo the paragraph's topic sentence in some way, much as the beginning and ending of the whole text often form a pair of bookends (see 1.2.4). The point is illustrated in Extracts 2.15 to 2.17, in which only the topic and final sentences of each paragraph

---

3   Text inside square brackets indicates a spoken form.

are shown. For instance, the last sentence of Extract 2.15 is a conclusion to the preceding argument (note the *thus*) with clear references to the topic sentence (*taking action during crisis* echoes *managing crises*, and *trade-off* reflects *dilemma*).

FINAL SENTENCES THAT ECHO THE TOPIC SENTENCE

Extract 2.15 [Maitlis & Christianson 2014: 85]
[Topic sentence:] Individuals and teams **managing crises** or unexpected events are faced with a **dilemma**. [...] [Final sentence:] **Taking action during crisis** thus involves a **trade-off** between "dangerous action which produces understanding and safe inaction which produces confusion" (Weick, 1988, p. 305).

Extract 2.16 [Shipp 2021: 336]
[Topic sentence:] As well as being a crucial time for the development of **national identity**, the long eighteenth century has always been seen as vital in the development of 'modern' **modes of cultural production**. [...] [Final sentence:] In this new climate, where literary works were **produced for a bourgeois 'public' or marketplace**, and where literature was associated with conceptions of British **identity** (rather than with the court), poets laureate became obsolescent.[1]

Extract 2.17 [Collinson 2020: 3]
[Topic sentence:] This neglect reflects the tendency in many studies to adopt **an excessively positive orientation** that treats power and control as unproblematic or unremarkable forms of organizational authority (Collinson, 2012). [...] [Final sentence:] **Studies typically take for granted that** (heroic) **leaders are invariably a source of good, that leaders'** efforts unfailingly produce **positive** outcomes and that the interests of **leaders** and followers invariably coalesce.

Similarly, in Extract 2.16, the topic sentence establishes a parallel between the development of *national identity* and of *'modern' modes of cultural production*, which is then reflected in the final sentence. Extract 2.17 ends with a different type of echo. Its final sentence provides three examples of the main idea introduced in the topic sentence (the *excessively positive orientation* of much research). In doing so, incidentally, it adds emphasis by making use of the so-called 'rule of three': the idea that sets of three elements are somehow more effective than other types of combination.

And one last point: just like topic sentences, final ones often play an important cohesive role. That is, they can help to connect the paragraph they end to the one that follows. The point will be discussed further in Section 5.3.

2.3 Paragraph appeal

If you've already done a reasonable amount of writing, you will probably have had the following experience. You design a paragraph rigorously in line with the principles we have outlined. The topic sentence states clearly the main idea, which is then meticulously developed; the final sentence refers back to the topic sentence, rounding things off nicely. And yet … Somehow there is no spark, nothing to really appeal to the reader. Of course, that may well be at least partly because the paragraph's own components, the individual sentences of which it is made up, themselves lack appeal (a matter for the next chapter). But it may also derive, just as it can at text level (see 1.3), from a lack of variety in the openings and lengths of those components.

This time we will reverse the order of discussion and begin with the question of sentence length. There is nothing inherently wrong with long sentences, a point we will discuss in Chapter 3. But a long series of them, however well managed, will overload your readers' capacity to process them. On the other hand, while short sentences are definitely a key element of good writing, stringing several together can easily sound clumsy and boring, causing readers to lose interest and perhaps also to doubt your competence. In other words, both long and short sentences are not just perfectly acceptable; they are necessary. What really matters is that they are interspersed with one another. The next example shows how this can work.

PARAGRAPH WITH VARIED SENTENCE LENGTHS
Extract 2.18 [Scales 2022: 334]
The narrative of Latin Europe's strengthening political divisions, and of their reflection in the medieval political-cultural imagination, has traditionally been recounted more in parallel than in conjunction with accounts of advancing cultural integration. **Some crossovers have, it is true, long been acknowledged and studied.** The new learning benefited State(s) hardly less than Church, whether through the increasingly systematic study of law, the application to secular government of

other useful sciences, or the stream of future bureaucrats turned out by the schools and universities.[74] **Yet the cultural traffic has often been presented as piecemeal, limited and one-way.** The '[high] medieval origins of the Modern State',[75] with its now-familiar counterpart, the 'emergence of European nations in the Middle Ages',[76] still constitutes a largely separate historiographical track, standing apart from the high medieval 'making of Europe' as a cultural phenomenon.

This example paragraph consists of six sentences, four of which (including the last, omitted here for reasons of space) are quite lengthy. However, they are broken up by two much shorter sentences (highlighted), both of which have simple, easy-to-follow structures. Without that variety, the paragraph would have been considerably less digestible – and far less appealing.

The second form of variety, in sentence openings, is nicely illustrated in Extract 2.19; in fact, all of its seven sentences begin differently.[4]

PARAGRAPH WITH VARIED SENTENCE OPENINGS
Extract 2.19 [Howlett 2022: 398–399]
Although one of the main benefits of field research is [...]. **In fact**, the virus has, [...]. **While** it may have previously been [...]. **As** this paper has outlined, mediated approaches can generate [...]. **Online fieldwork** can also grant us access to [...]. **In extending a field site** in time and space [...]. **Accordingly**, reaching the field no longer requires [...].

Just imagine that the beginnings of this paragraph's sentences had looked like this, as they could have done without distorting the overall message in any way.

- *The COVID-19 pandemic has made field research ...*
- *The virus has, in fact, pushed us back into the armchair ...*
- *Accessing participants in our field sites may ...*
- *Mediated approaches can generate valuable insight ...*
- *Online fieldwork can also grant us access to ...*
- *Extending a field site ...*
- *Reaching the field thus no longer requires ...*

---

4   In this extract, only the sentence openings are shown. We will examine the full paragraph in Section 3.4.2.

The repetitiveness of form is almost audible. But such repetition cannot be resolved simply at the word level. It can only be avoided if you have at your disposal a variety of different sentence structures. It is to such structures that we will turn in Chapter 3.

Chapter 2: The takeaways

- Paragraphs deal with a single main idea or a distinct aspect of an idea.
- They almost always consist of at least three sentences.
- They have no fixed maximum length, but they should not contain more information than readers can take in without opportunity for reflection.
- They are structured in line with fairly strict rules into three components:
  □ a topic sentence setting out the main idea
  □ one or more supporting sentences that develop that idea
  □ a final sentence that rounds the paragraph off
- The topic sentence also introduces key terminology that will recur in the paragraph's course.
- The development of the main idea is linear and takes place in a series of steps, so as to create a feeling of progress.
- This development can take a wide variety of forms depending on the topic, but two that can be used generally are:
  □ bulleted lists
  □ tables and figures integrated into the text
- The final sentence is typically the paragraph's climax in some sense, and often refers back to the topic sentence in order to bookend what comes between.
- Paragraph appeal can be increased by varying:
  □ sentence openings
  □ sentence lengths

3 *Focus and flow*:
Constructing sentences

God, let me think clearly and brightly;
let me live, love, and say it
well in good sentences.
Sᴜʟᴠɪᴀ Pʟᴀᴛʜ (1932 – 1963),
The Unabridged Journals of Sylvia Plath

"If you find that writing is hard", Zinsser reassures us, "it's because it is hard" (2006: 9). Nowhere does this become more apparent than at the level of the sentence, the third of our seven pillars. While larger text elements such as the paragraph or section also involve a number of difficult choices, most writers feel that the sentence level is where they face the biggest challenges. The decisions to be taken can be deceptively simple, yet agonisingly complex. What should the sentence be about, and how should it begin? What news does it convey, and where should the most interesting bits go? How much information can the sentence reasonably hold without making too many demands on the reader?

Ostensibly, these questions may not be about grammatical form, but about function, rhetoric and how information is arranged. Yet it is grammar that specifies what choices the writer has in the first place. And if writers make use of the full variety of available choices, their texts will be more effective: clearer, more precise, more dynamic and more attractive to readers. It follows that, although this chapter is not part of a grammar book, our audience would be ill served if we failed to explain a few basics here or there. We will do so on a need-to-know basis, bearing in mind what types of text researchers typically write and why. Accordingly, our approach is unapologetically pragmatic and selective.

3.1 Sentence types

Even if an academic writer is not interested in grammar *per se*, they will still find it useful to understand the basic types of sentence structure in order to employ them effectively and creatively. In this section, we will outline those types and briefly discuss their uses in research papers. In doing so, we will also introduce the important but slippery concept of a 'clause'.

3.1.1 The simple sentence

In a book on academic English, a section on the *simple* sentence may seem oddly out of place. Surely research is a *complex* affair? True, but it is the underlying ideas that should be complex, not the way they are expressed. In English, you earn no praise for using tangled structures to parade your brilliance. Instead, you are meant to focus readers' attention on the substance of the message rather than its form. That is where the simple sentence comes into its own.

A simple sentence contains a subject and a so-called 'finite' verb form: that is, a verb form which matches the subject in person (1st, 2nd or 3rd) and number (singular or plural), and indicates the tense (present simple, past continuous and so on). An example would be *The method works*. A simple sentence may also contain an object, a complement, adjectives, adverbs or adverbial phrases: for instance, *Surprisingly, the new method works brilliantly most of the time.* And that's it. For a sentence to remain a simple one, we cannot add any further clauses (i.e., elements that include a verb of any shape or form). Here are a few authentic examples of simple sentences.

SIMPLE SENTENCES
Extract 3.1 [Tiersma 1999: 1]
Our law is a law of words.

Extract 3.2 [Collinson 2020: 6]
Importantly, Foucault also highlighted the dialectical relationship between power and resistance.

Extract 3.3 [Parker 2018: 187]
I don't agree.

As Extracts 3.1 to 3.3 show, simple sentences tend to be short, but that need not be the case. The sentence in Extract 3.4 is simple but consists of 21 words, and some are significantly longer than that.

A SIMPLE BUT RELATIVELY LONG SENTENCE
Extract 3.4 [Piekkari, Welch & Westney 2022: 6][1]
Both bodies of work focus on a level of analysis above or below the level of the MNC as an organization.

The examples provided so far are all so-called declarative sentences, which are typically used to make statements. They are the most common sentence type in academic discourse. Yet in English academic writing, it is not uncommon to find interrogative sentences that ask (rhetorical) questions.

A QUESTION IN ACADEMIC WRITING
Extract 3.5 [MacDowell 2018: 276]
In order to explain ironic expression in film, then, perhaps we need not speak of "meanings" at all, but only of the various perspectives or attitudes that a film can imply. **However, can irony really exist without any concept of "surface meaning" at all?**

---

1   *MNC = multinational corporation*

Rarer, but not unknown are imperative sentences (i.e., those that ostensibly give an instruction).

AN INSTRUCTION IN ACADEMIC WRITING
Extract 3.6 [Taylor 2020: 173]
For instance, social categories associated with trends are often very fragile. **Consider** the cases of the beatnik and the football casual.

As noted above, simple sentences cannot contain any other clauses. It is possible, though, to form what is known as a *compound sentence* by combining two or more simple ones. This can be done in two different ways. The first is to use one of the so-called 'fanboys' (i.e., those conjunctions that can connect either whole sentences or parts of the same sentence): *for, and, nor, but, or, yet* and *so*. Extract 3.7 provides an example. Alternatively, the close connection may be established by a semi-colon rather than a full stop (see Extract 3.8). A comma cannot be used unless the compound sentence consists of more than two short main clauses, as in *I came, I saw,* [and] *I conquered.*

COMPOUND SENTENCES
Extract 3.7 [Collinson 2020: 10]
Senior positions typically confer greater autonomy, status and privilege, **but** they may also nurture leaders' hubris, narcissism and arrogance (Sadler-Smith, 2019; Tourish, 2020).

Extract 3.8 [Gray & Gray 2011: 30]
In this context, property questions are profound; their reach is universal; their power to engage is immense.

To sum up: simple sentences are a vital tool in academic writing. Thanks to their lack of complexity, and the fact that they tend to be short, they can be processed easily by readers and so prove very effective. If phrased as questions or instructions, they help to structure the argument, and do so in a manner that appears to directly address the reader. As a result, they make the text both clearer and more engaging.

3.1.2 The complex sentence

Impressive as they are, these virtues of simple sentences do not mean that academic writing can rely solely on them. Not only, as we remarked in Section 2.3, would that make for unappealing paragraphs, and thus unappealing texts. Just as importantly, writers need a vehicle for expressing, in a precise and nuanced way, complex relations between ideas that are themselves often complex – a need that simple sentences alone cannot meet. Hence the requirement for complex sentences in all their various forms.

So what do we mean by a *complex sentence*? The term doesn't just refer to any sentence that seems to us, personally, a bit complicated; it has a specific grammatical meaning. In that sense, a complex sentence contains several clauses which are in some way dependent on one another. One clause – and only one – could stand on its own as a separate grammatical sentence; this is termed the *main clause*. The remainder, those which could not, are termed *subordinate* (or *dependent*) *clauses*.

Each of Extracts 3.9 to 3.11 consists of a complex sentence. The first contains a single subordinate clause (*although ...*), whereas the two others contain several. In Extract 3.10 these begin with *since* and *while*, in Extract 3.11 with *developing, as* and *so that*. In this last example, all three subordinate clauses follow the main clause; in the other two, the sentence begins with a subordinate clause.

> COMPLEX SENTENCES
> **Extract 3.9** [Sofaer et al. 2021: 1129]
> **Although** heritage is widely understood as a common good, over recent decades the sector has become increasingly concerned with having to account for itself and the value of heritage to society.
>
> **Extract 3.10** [Collinson 2020: 6]
> **Since** asymmetrical power relations are always two-way, leaders will to some extent remain dependent on the led, **while** the latter retain a degree of autonomy and discretion.
>
> **Extract 3.11** [Shaw & Bailey 2009: 416]
> Discourse analytic studies often start with a general problem area, **developing** more focused research questions **as** the research progresses **so that** researchers can remain genuinely open to new insights.

It is possible for complex sentences to be as short as simple ones. The one shown in the next extract has not just one but two subordinate clauses (*that ...*; *of which*), but has the same number of words, 21, as the simple sentence in Extract 3.4 above. As a rule, though, complex sentences are longer than simple ones.

A COMPLEX BUT RELATIVELY SHORT SENTENCE
Extract 3.12 [Bouvier & Machin 2021: 313]
The danger therefore in individualising racism and xenophobia is **that** we miss these wider patterns **of which** it is a part.

But how long may complex sentences legitimately be? There seems to be a general consensus that English sentences should not be too lengthy, or indeed too complex. Hence supervisors and reviewers often suggest – or demand – "split in two". But neither they nor anyone else can define exactly when a sentence becomes too long or too complex; the answer depends on many different factors.

The fact is that neither sentence length nor complexity is a problem *per se*; however, both increase the onus on the writer to help the reader. "Your aim", Moran (2018: 41) reminds us, "is to clear a path for the reader, a way through the sentence that will not get her lost." This path can be obscured for a number of reasons, the following among them.

- It is not immediately obvious what pronouns such as *it* or *their* refer to (see 5.2.2).
- Punctuation is unhelpful or downright misleading (see Chapter 4).
- The subject and the verb are too far apart.
- Dependent clauses are embedded (i.e., placed inside) one another in a way that makes it difficult for the reader to see how things hang together.

Makeover 3.1 illustrates what can happen when flaws of the last two types occur, and also the sort of measures that can help to avoid them.

MAKEOVER 3.1: CLEARING THE LINGUISTIC PATH
Before
The question to be resolved, which generations of researchers have been asking and has yet to be satisfactorily answered, is whether a categorisation that clearly distinguishes between these two types of situation is feasible.

After
For generations, researchers have been debating a tricky question that still lacks a satisfactory answer: is it feasible to draw up a categorisation that clearly distinguishes between these two types of situation?

In the Makeover's *Before* sentence, the subject (*the question to be resolved*) is separated by no less than 14 words from the verb (*is*), which itself provides the weakest of connections between two weighty sentence halves. Moreover, the *that*-clause in the second half is embedded within the clause that begins with *whether*. As a result, readers are sent, not along a simple path, but on a scramble through a tangled linguistic web.

In the *After* sentence, by contrast, the reader's path has been noticeably cleared. The subordinate clause starting with *which* has been made into a main clause unencumbered by dependent ones, bringing subject and verb right next to each other (*researchers have been debating*). The remainder of the sentence has been converted into a direct question, separated off appropriately by a colon (see 4.2.2). What is more, the question's two subordinate clauses (*to draw up …; that …*) are not embedded; instead, the second follows on from the first. The resulting improvement in information flow is plain to see. And it has been achieved without lengthening the sentence, which now actually has two words fewer than before (32 as against 34).

It is clearly impossible to lay down general rules for keeping sentences manageable. What we can say, though, is that the longer and more complex a sentence becomes, the more important it is to observe the principles set out in Toolbox 3.1.

> **Toolbox 3.1**
> **CLEARING THE LINGUISTIC PATH THROUGH SENTENCES**
>
> - Create a clear, linear structure with little or no embedding of clauses.
> - Make references unambiguous (through pronouns, for example).
> - Establish internal coherence and cohesion (see Chapter 5).
> - Use punctuation marks to indicate clearly which elements belong together, and where the reader should pause (see Chapter 4).

3.1.3 Subordinate clauses

The examples of complex sentences we have given so far will have offered a glimpse of just how varied subordinate clauses can be. For reasons of focus as much as of space, we will not elaborate on the specifics of their structure and function here, so for a more detailed account we would recommend turning to an advanced grammar book such as Hewings (2013). What we will do, however, is comment briefly on the most important types of dependent clause.

Relative clauses

Relative clauses are introduced by relative pronouns (*that, which, who, whose, of which* etc.) and come in two types. The first is a defining relative clause, so called because it defines a preceding noun. Extract 3.13 provides an example; note the absence of commas before the relative pronoun *that* (see 4.3.1).

> **A 'DEFINING' RELATIVE CLAUSE**
> **Extract 3.13** [McLean 2021: 473]
> It would not be surprising were scholars to focus upon these events, but this would risk overlooking other not-insignificant developments **that** are occurring in plain sight.

The second type of relative clause does not define a preceding noun, but provides additional information about it, as in the following example. In this case, as you can see, the clause is indeed 'commaed off'.

A 'NON-DEFINING' RELATIVE CLAUSE
Extract 3.14 [Gross 2022: 451]
This hostility of neoliberalism to political imagination and action is a starting point for Lynne Segal's (2017) *Radical Happiness*, **in which** she argues that it is in the recovery of the pleasures of collective experience – in defiance of systemic individualism – that we can reclaim the space for new politics.

Object clauses
Other subordinate clauses function as objects (and are called *object clauses*). They are most typically introduced by *that* or *whether*. Extracts 3.15 and 3.16 provide examples. Again, note the absence of commas (see 4.3.1).

OBJECT CLAUSES WITH *THAT* AND *WHETHER*
Extract 3.15 [Tinsley 2022: 245]
They argued **that** the origin of the crisis lay in discourses, among them "capitalism, extractivism, racism, sexism, classism, and ableism".

Extract 3.16 [Flaim & Blaisdell 2020: 1177]
As each item is presented, the participant must decide **whether** it matches an item presented n trials ago, with the range typically extending from 0–3 (Jaeggi, Buschkuehl, Jonides, & Perrig, 2008).

However, an object clause may also be introduced by any of the so-called *wh*-words used to ask questions: *what, why, how*, etc.

OBJECT CLAUSES WITH *WH*-WORDS
Extract 3.17 [Harris & Leeming 2022: 18-19]
Perhaps if students had understood **why** they were being asked to speak before any focus on language, they would have been more positive about the approach and their own learning.

Extract 3.18 [Schumpe et al. 2018: 549]
The present research demonstrates **how** support for political violence can be reduced by providing peaceful alternatives to produce social change.

Adverbial clauses

Next comes a varied array of what are known as *adverbial clauses*. The most common types are set out in Table 3.1, along with some of the words and expressions that typically introduce them.

Clause type	Typical introductions
Time	*when; as; while*
Cause	*because; as; since*
Purpose	*so that; so as to; in order to; in order that; to*
Condition	*if; provided (that); supposing (that); unless*
Contrast	*while; whereas*
Concession	*although; though; even if; even though; despite the fact that*
Manner	*as; just as; as though; as if*

Table 3.1 Common adverbial clause types with their typical introductions

The next five extracts provide examples of some of these clause types. The first shows a clause of purpose and the second a clause of contrast, while the last three all include clauses of concession.

ASSORTED ADVERBIAL CLAUSES

Extract 3.19 [Manata & Bozeman 2022: 337]
To justify the aggregation of individual-level scores to the group level of analysis, within-group agreement in subject responses was analyzed.

Extract 3.20 [Townley 2021: 547]
While the email genre illustrated in Table 2 is designed to provide the client with an explanatory account of negotiation activity, the emails represented in Tables 3–5 were used by the legal and business professionals to collaborate on proposed amendments to the intertextual wording of the legal documents.

Extract 3.21 [Munno et al. 2022: 66]
That is to not say we will necessarily have students complete the Q sort every semester, **although** we found that it generated productive discussion.

Extract 3.22 [Jones, H. 2019: 198]
During the Commonwealth, **although** there were imperial conflicts and conquests in the Caribbean, far more attention was paid by Cromwell to the establishment of a united British Isles, largely due to the need to supress royalists and Catholics in Scotland and Ireland.

Extract 3.23 [Chambers & Berger-Walliser 2021: 594]
Even if domestic law accepts human rights violations as a basis for an actionable private claim, due to the variety of international human rights instruments, it is currently unclear which human rights this will affect.

Extracts 3.21 and 3.22 also illustrate how an adverbial clause need not come at the start of a sentence. In the former it is preceded by the main clause, in the latter by an initial adverbial phrase that relates to the sentence as a whole.

Participle clauses
Despite what we said above, there is one type of clause that we would like to comment on in rather more detail: the participle clause. Two varieties can be distinguished, depending on whether the clause is introduced by a present participle (with -*ing*) or by a past participle (with -*ed* if the verb is regular, and various other forms if it is irregular). The following passage, taken from an abstract, includes one example of each variety.

PARTICIPLE CLAUSES AS ALTERNATIVES TO FULL SENTENCES
Extract 3.24 [Skukauskaite, Trout & Robinson 2021: 403]
Building on the growing field of utilizing arts-based practices in teaching qualitative research, in this article we examine how one doctoral student's engagement with drawing and painting within and beyond a qualitative research class supported her developing reflexivity. **Guided** by an interactional ethnographic perspective, we conducted domain, taxonomic, and discourse analyses of the student's art, reflection journals, video of a class presentation, and retrospective reflections she wrote three years later.

In this extract, the first sentence could have been written as a compound sentence with two main clauses (*we build on ..., and we examine ...*).

Beginning with a participle clause enables the authors to establish a closer connection between the two actions ('building' and 'examining') without specifying the nature of the link. Much the same applies to the past participle (*guided*) in the second sentence.

Quite frequently, a participle clause offers a more compact and less intrusive alternative to a relative clause. This type of situation is illustrated in Extracts 3.25 and 3.26. Once again, the absence of commas is worth noting (see 4.3.1).

PARTICIPLE CLAUSES AS ALTERNATIVES TO RELATIVE CLAUSES

Extract 3.25 [Fleming 2021: 4-5]
The following section thus sets out a theory **linking** prime ministers' electoral success to their ability to conduct post-election cabinet re-shuffles.

Extract 3.26 [Spence 2021: 1]
After introducing the benefits and potential problems **brought about** by the digital economy, I then discuss the important role of government in ensuring that the digital economy functions properly.

In other cases, participle clauses help us avoid cumbersome constructions involving abstract nouns attached to *of*-phrases. This capacity is a real asset in English, a language that relies heavily on verbs "to bring sentences to life" (Moran 2018: 46; see 3.4.1). Thus, the participle *using*, for example, makes for a more light-footed version of *through the use of*, just as *developing* can stand in for *due to the development of*, and so on.

To sum up, participle clauses are useful devices for several reasons. Linking clauses smoothly and unobtrusively, they add variety and help avoid heavy abstract nouns (see 3.4.1 for the stylistic benefits). Participle clauses are not even especially complicated. Yet there is one area where they can prove tricky (for native and non-native writers alike). That is because, for a participle clause to work, its implicit subject should be identical with the explicit subject of the main clause. In Extract 3.24 the subject of *building* – implied but not mentioned – is *we*, and it is also *we* that functions as the subject of the ensuing main clause (*we examine*); likewise, the implicit subject of *guided*, again *we*, is picked up in the main clause (*we conducted*).

Although this seems self-evident, it can easily be overlooked. Consider this (invented) sentence: *Refining these methods, the research design was im-*

proved. Taken literally, this says that it was the research design that refined the methods, when of course it was actually the researchers themselves that did the refining, which then led to the improvement. To make that clear, the sentence would have to be rewritten along these lines: *Refining / By refining these methods, we improved the research design.* In practice, the likelihood of misunderstanding may not be high, but like other seemingly minor types of error, such 'dangling' participles can significantly disrupt readers' processing of a text.

Finally, like all devices, participle clauses should be used in moderation. Otherwise, their positive impact is soon lost so that the text sounds repetitive and boring. And sometimes, of course, a 'heavier' alternative, such as a full relative clause with *which*, is exactly what a particular sentence needs in order to be clear and well-balanced.

3.2 Principles of sentence construction

Now that we have introduced simple and complex sentences, it is time to turn to the basic principles underlying their strategic construction. These principles are the basis on which a writer establishes an appropriate 'flow' of information, so that each item follows as naturally as possible from the one before. There are two such precepts, and we will discuss them in turn.

3.2.1 The 'given-new' principle

The first key precept is known as the *given-new principle,* or sometimes as the *information principle* (Biber et al. 1999: 896). It is very simple and provides three pieces of sound advice. The first is that sentences should start with an item of information with which readers are already familiar, either from their own knowledge and experience, or because it has previously been introduced in the text. We could say that the start of the sentence is the take-off-point for the flight ahead.

The second piece of advice is to add new information progressively as the sentence proceeds. In other words, each item should build on those that have come before. To continue with our metaphor, the sentence's middle is its flight path, which must be as smooth as possible if the flight is to end well.

Thirdly, the given-new principle states that the end of the sentence, where it touches down, should bring something new, not more of what is already familiar. A flight that merely returns to the departure point doesn't bring any progress. And progress is what the reader needs to feel.

The sort of thing that can result from violating the given-new principle is illustrated in the *Before* sentence of Makeover 3.2. There, *data* has the status of known information since it appears near the beginning. The problem is that it also appears at the sentence's end, giving readers the impression that, far from making any progress, they have gone round in a circle.

MAKEOVER 3.2: OBSERVING THE GIVEN-NEW PRINCIPLE

Before

Brown and Smith (2021) use data from four different museums and develop a groundbreaking theoretical model on the basis of these data.

After

Using data from four different museums, Brown and Smith (2020) develop a groundbreaking theoretical model.

The *After* sentence shows the type of action that may be required to make sure that the principle is observed. In it, *data* has been confined to the early part of the sentence, where it belongs, by including it in a separate participle clause (*Using data ...*). That in turn has left the end position free for the new information, the *groundbreaking theoretical model*. As a result, information flows smoothly and a sense of progress is established.

In Extract 3.27, the second sentence provides an authentic example. Taking off from *affirming programming*, it then gives two instances of such programming (*social and support groups*) before touching down on new information: the two potential positive results of such programmes.

THE GIVEN-NEW PRINCIPLE IN ACTION

Extract 3.27 [Gillig, Macary & Gross 2022: 326]

From a practical standpoint, our findings suggest the need for pro-gramming and **policies affirming** LGBTQ family identity. **Affirming programming**, such as social and support groups, can provide LGBTQ parents with a respite from social challenges and can demonstrate to their children that many other families like theirs exist.

This extract also illustrates how the given-new principle applies, not only within sentences, but also across their boundaries and beyond. The take-off point of the sentence we have just discussed (*affirming programming*) wasn't chosen at random; it is precisely where the preceding sentence landed (*policies affirming LGBTQ family identity*). The same applies to the first sentence of the extract, since both information items mentioned at its start (*a practical standpoint* and *our findings*) are picked up from the preceding paragraph (not quoted here), which discusses theoretical implications of the study's results. This sort of connection facilitates the smooth flow of information through paragraphs and even whole texts, and is a standard feature of good academic writing. If the connections are interrupted at some point, perhaps because of a switch to consider a new aspect of the idea under discussion, then that must be announced to the reader by means of suitable metacomments (see 7.1).

3.2.2 End focus

The second key guide to sentence construction is the principle of end focus. This states that, in English, the end of a clause or sentence receives comparatively more attention than the rest. This is why you need to reserve that spot for the really interesting bits which you want the reader to focus on. If you succeed, the sentence builds up to a sort of climax at its end. If you fail, emphasis is given to something you did not in fact consider worth emphasising, and the reader's attention is misdirected.

The principle is illustrated in Extract 3.28, in which the important and interesting information is not *the composition of the final bouquet*, but the *performer*. Accordingly, the *composition* is placed at the beginning of the *but*-clause, and the *performer* at the end, where it will get all the attention.

END FOCUS IN ACTION
Extract 3.28 [Loges 2021: 20]
To use another metaphor often found on the frontispieces of [song] collections, the composer proffered a selection of flowers, but the composition of the final bouquet was left to the performer.

To sum up, end focus is what enables a writer to arouse readers' curiosity, maintain their interest and draw their attention to the elements that the writer considers most important. Without it, sentences or series of sentences lack any feeling of drama; they remain bland and fall distinctly flat. Regrettably, end focus is all too often ignored – even in much academic writing. In Makeover 3.3, we illustrate the damaging effects this can have, and how they can be eliminated.

MAKEOVER 3.3: RESTORING END FOCUS

Before

The team that made this breakthrough followed it up with a series of other major discoveries rather than resting on their laurels as they could so easily have done.

After

Rather than resting on their laurels as they could so easily have done, the team that made this breakthrough followed it up with a series of other major discoveries.

In this case, unlike the one discussed in Makeover 3.2, the issue is less that the information placed at the end of the *Before* sentence (*rather than resting ... could so easily have done*) is already known to the reader (indeed the latter part might be seen as a statement of the obvious). Nor does *the team that ...* provide an inappropriate take-off point since it has clearly been mentioned previously. The problem is that the new information is pretty boring, and certainly not what the writer intended to highlight. A climax it is not.

This problem is resolved in the *After* sentence. Instead of being buried in the middle of the sentence attracting no particular attention, the sentence's key message (*major discoveries*), appears in the precious end position. The sentence has gone out, not with a whimper but with a loud bang.

Of course, despite the distinction drawn between Makeovers 3.2 and 3.3, end focus is closely related to the given-new principle. Moran (2018: 119) again sums up matters nicely: "A plain English sentence moves smoothly and easily towards its final point. The best way to ensure this happens is to put the important stuff at the end."

3.3 Passive sentences

Although we do not intend here to delve into the great boxful of English sentence structures, there is one that cannot be left unmentioned: the passive sentence. One of its uses is illustrated in Extract 3.28 above, where it is the passive form *was left* that enables end focus to be established. That is possible because the passive voice moves the agent of an action (i.e., the 'doer') from its position at (or at least near) the start of a sentence to its end. Thus, the active sentence *The dog bit the postman*, which emphasises who the dog bit, can become *The postman was bitten by the dog* (and not, for example, by the neighbour's pet puma). The active sentence answers the question *What did the dog do?*, whereas the passive responds to *What happened to the postman?*

Yet, despite its merits, there is no denying that the passive generally gets a bad press. 'Avoid the passive' is a popular mantra in training courses, style guides and self-help books 'for the successful communicator', populist texts which often seek to bolster their arguments by citing that master essayist George Orwell. And it is perfectly true that the fourth of his *Six Rules for Writing* [2] begins *Never use the passive.* What the anti-passive brigade generally ignore, however, is that the rule continues with the very significant qualification *where you can use the active.* Moreover, Orwell's sixth and final rule is a universal escape clause: *Break any of these rules sooner than say anything outright barbarous.* Indeed, in the essay from which the quotation comes, Orwell himself uses the passive a number of times – when it is the appropriate choice. So to suggest that he favoured a simplistic, blanket ban on passivisation is a gross distortion. It is actually much more likely that he would have concurred with what Moran (2018: 68) has to say about ill-informed "censure" of the passive voice: "Skilled writers ignore it."

In fact, the importance of the passive extends well beyond its key role in ensuring end focus. It is, for instance, the structure of choice when the phrase that describes the agent is too long to make a comfortable subject. Unlike German, say, English does not take kindly to top-heavy sentences. The subject needs to be short, whereas the predicate – that is, the verb and everything that follows it – can be long: a principle referred to as *end weight.* As Biber et al. (1999) explain, end weight often works in tandem with the given-new principle (see 3.2.1); together, they help the reader process the information presented.

---

2   Included in his essay *Politics and the English Language* (Orwell [1946] 2013).

There is a preferred distribution of elements in the clause in accordance with their weight called the principle of end-weight: the tendency for long and complex elements to be placed towards the end of a clause. This eases comprehension by the receiver, who does not then have the burden of retaining complex information from earlier in a clause in short-term memory while processing the remainder. Since heavy elements typically also carry a substantial new information load, the information principle and the principle of end-weight often reinforce one another (p. 898).

In the following extract, we can see the passive being used in the service of both end weight and end focus. The *by*-phrase specifying the agent (emboldened in the example) would be far too unwieldy as a subject, and a straightforward conversion from passive to active would make the sentence extremely top-heavy.

THE PASSIVE, END-WEIGHT AND END FOCUS
Extract 3.29 [Lipson 2013: 220]
The field of Egyptology has been intrigued by **an ancient Egyptian pharaoh named Akhenaten, from the fourteenth century BCE, who attempted large-scale ideological, religious, political, and rhetorical changes – only to be erased from history until the nineteenth century**.

Such structural issues are by no means the only good reasons for using a passive form. Others relate to the availability of information about the agent of a particular action. If the agent is unknown, then a passive form is usually the only option. But even if a writer is aware of an agent's identity, they may not wish to introduce that information explicitly into their text because it seems to be unimportant, irrelevant, or for some other motive (e.g., for reasons of confidentiality). And sometimes the agent may be so self-evident that mentioning it or them explicitly would seem unnecessary and possibly patronising.

In one particular area of academic writing, that is so often the case that the passive voice is not just useful but absolutely indispensable: in Methods sections. There, it allows writers to avoid clumsy strings of sentences all beginning with *I* or *we*: agents, in other words, that are implied and need not be made explicit. The following is a typical example.

THE PASSIVE IN A METHODS SECTION

Extract 3.30 [Thomas 2021: 696]

Participants **were invited** to take part in a face-to-face interview in a location of their choosing. On two occasions, interviews **were carried out** by phone due to their stated preference. Twenty of the participants were in a relationship (10 couples) and **were interviewed** as a couple (all requested this). [...] I informed participants that they can withdraw at any time, stop the audio-recorder at any moment, and avoid answering certain questions. They **were told** that their data **would be kept** confidential and safe, and I would make every attempt to ensure that anonymity **is preserved** (pseudonyms **have been provided**).

This does not mean, of course, that such sections include no active sentences at all; in fact, Extract 3.30 shows how a good mix between the passive and the active voice (*I informed ...; I would make every attempt*) adds variety and makes the text livelier. And not only that: with some methods, such as in-depth, face-to-face interviews, the demographics of the interviewer (their age, ethnicity, social class, etc.) can interact with those of the interviewees, so that it makes a big difference who actually carries out the interview in the field. In such cases, using the passive consistently and never revealing who the interviewer was would be a methodological flaw rather than a linguistic one. So in Extract 3.30 the author's choice to use *I* several times is likely to have been a substantive rather than merely a stylistic choice.

In Brief
THE USES OF THE PASSIVE

Far from being inappropriate or even an 'error', the passive voice is of crucial importance in academic writing because:

- It facilitates the establishment of end focus, smooth information flow and end weight;
- It enables writers to deal with unknown agents, and to suppress an agent's identity if they so wish;
- It prevents Methods sections from becoming unbearably repetitive.

3.4 Sentence appeal

So far in this chapter, our focus has been on how sentences can be structured and how they can perform certain functions, such as emphasising particular items of information. But we have said little about sentences within the context of paragraphs, or about possible ways of making your sentences, alone or in the company of others, more attractive to readers. In the remainder of this section, we will offer some thoughts and advice about two areas crucial for the construction of appealing sentences.

3.4.1 Getting the verb-noun balance right

The first of these areas concerns the two fundamental building blocks of English sentences: nouns and verbs. Moran (2018: 82) describes them as "the two poles of the sentence. Nouns keep it still; verbs make it move". Between these poles there is an inevitable tension that writers must resolve by striking the right balance.

It seems to be generally agreed that English is above all a 'verby' language. Verbs are what "bring sentences to life" (Moran 2018: 46). But that is not to say there is anything wrong with nouns as such; what matters is the type of nouns and how they are used. Consider this sentence: *In our second experiment, the microphone was placed on the table, and the toys on the floor in front of the children.* It contains six nouns, all of them concrete, referring as they do to people and things. They pose no difficulty for the reader, and the same goes for concrete nouns in general.

The problems start when we leave the realm of the concrete, as is illustrated in Makeover 3.4.

MAKEOVER 3.4: AVOIDING ABSTRACT NOUNS
Before
The application of the theory led to the realisation that the selection of the right methods mix was of the utmost importance.

After
Once we applied the theory, we realised that selecting the right methods mix was vitally important.

In the *Before* sentence, the reader is confronted by three nouns (*application*, *realisation* and *selection*) which are so-called nominalisations – that is, abstract nouns based on verbs (in this case *apply, realise* and *select*). Nominalisations leave the reader with a sense of vagueness, and the stylistic appeal is further reduced because the nouns need to be strung together with a series of rather bland prepositions, *of* in particular. In this sentence, a further abstract noun (*importance*) plays an adjectival role, requiring a further preposition, again *of*, to be added to the plethora.

In the *After* sentence, by contrast, these problems are resolved by transforming these nouns into the word class whose roles they had been imitating. Thus the first three have been converted back into verb forms (*applied, realised, selecting*), removing the need for at least some prepositions. And the fourth has been replaced with an adjective (*important*). As a result, not an *of* is to be seen, the readers know exactly who did what, and the sentence has been given a variety it previously lacked – and so becomes considerably more appealing. Just as Moran suggests, the *After* version definitely sounds livelier than the *Before* one. The key message, as Sword (2012: 173) reminds us, is the following: "Concrete language is the stylish writer's magic bullet". Abstract language, on the other hand, can cause problems and needs to be handled with care.

However, we would not want to phrase this advice more categorically. For, in research, abstraction does play a key role. Without it, scholars could not do their job, which consists not only in observing the world around them but also in distilling general principles from what they see. In academic discourse, accordingly, abstract nouns are indispensable. Thus, what we mean by handling them 'with care' is that writers should use as few of them as possible – but, by all means, as many as necessary.

3.4.2 Varying sentence structure

In the previous subsection, we suggested that sentences are more appealing if they use an appropriate variety of verbs and nouns (and among nouns, of concrete and abstract ones). Variety is also the spice of life when it comes to deciding which types of clause to use. We will round off the chapter by looking at how sentences can also be made more varied in that sense.

To do so, we will return to an example we discussed in the previous chapter (repeated here in full as Extract 3.31). There we were interested in the paragraph appeal generated by the fact that all the constituent sentences have different openings. Here, we will focus on the positive effects created by using a broad range of clause types throughout the paragraph.

VARIED CLAUSE TYPES WITHIN A PARAGRAPH

Extract 3.31 [Howlett 2022: 398-399]

Although one of the main benefits of field research is gathering first-hand experience by getting out of the 'armchair' and entering the sites under study, the COVID-19 pandemic has made this methodological approach incredibly difficult. In fact, the virus has, in many ways, pushed us back *into* the armchair—both in a physical and metaphorical sense—and required us to utilize new methods to conduct research from our own homes. While it may have previously been more difficult to access participants in our field sites, advancements in technology have allowed for new armchair approaches to interact with our participants, and even glimpse into their daily lives, from afar. As this paper has outlined, mediated approaches can generate valuable insight not otherwise available through the use of in-person methods which may actually be richer and more insightful, especially when discussing personal or sensitive topics (Jenner and Myers, 2019). Online fieldwork can also grant us access to audiovisual data, introduce us to new networks, and assist us in engaging with our participants and local-level dynamics in ways that would not otherwise be possible. In extending a field site in time and space beyond a specific bounded online or offline site (Hine, 2015), mediated approaches thus offer a means of observing our field sites and establishing co-presence with participants with no loss of rapport or a reduction in intimacy (Jenner and Myers, 2019). Accordingly, reaching the field no longer requires entering it in a physical sense, just as 'returning from the field does not mean leaving the field in an absolute sense' (Knott, 2019: 148).

We will not list here all the different clause types used in this paragraph, but they include:

- Relative clauses (*which may actually ...; that would not otherwise ...*);
- Participle and gerund clauses (e.g., *especially when discussing ...; by getting out of ...; in engaging with ...*);
- An infinitive clause (*to interact with ...*);
- Several types of adverbial clause (e.g., *although one of ...; while it may have ...*).

If you use such a variety of structures, you add interest to the text and create a sense of forward movement. By contrast, sticking to the same syntactic pattern throughout a paragraph can quickly result in an unappealing humdrum rhythm, stomping rather than flowing. It is true that strings of sentences based on the same pattern can work, and work well, but only if there is a compelling rhetorical reason in favour of uniformity, such as the desire for cohesion (see 5.2.4) or emphasis. Otherwise, variety is the key.

At the same time, we would not wish to imply that 'variation' is a strict rule. However, there is no question that writers who are mindful in this regard, and who have a good understanding and command of the different clause types, produce more appealing texts: harder to write, it is true, but so much easier and more pleasurable to read. And therefore much more likely to have the desired impact on their readers.

Chapter 3: The takeaways

- Simple sentences consist of a single clause; they are thus easily processed and very effective in academic writing.
- Complex sentences consist of a single main clause and one or more subordinate clauses. They are needed to express more complex ideas, but in using them writers must ensure that a clear linguistic path runs through them.
- A good mix of simple and complex sentences is essential.
- Subordinate clauses come in a number of varieties, three of the most common being relative, object and adverbial clauses.
- Participle clauses are particularly useful; they can:
  - establish a close connection between two actions
  - offer a more compact alternative to relative clauses
  - help to avoid clumsy constructions involving abstract nouns and prepositions.
- Well-constructed sentences respect the 'given-new' principle and the need for end focus.
- Passive sentences are not bad in themselves. In fact, they are an essential tool of effective writing because, among other reasons, they:
  - enable end focus to be maintained
  - allow writers to deal with unknown, irrelevant and self-evident agents
- Two good ways of making sentences more appealing are by:
  - maintaining a good balance of nouns and verbs
  - varying their length and structure

4 *Breath marks*:
Punctuation

> *Yesterday Mr. Hall wrote that the printer's*
> *proof-reader was improving my punctua-*
> *tion for me, & I telegraphed orders to have*
> *him shot without giving him time to pray.*
> MARK TWAIN (1835 – 1910)

The significance of punctuation is easily underrated. After all, researchers deal in big ideas; so why worry about such small things? This view is seriously misguided. Small though they are, punctuation marks help writers present their thoughts clearly and compellingly, and our first task in this chapter will be to explain why that is so.

If punctuation matters, then that raises the next question: what precisely is the purpose of the various individual punctuation marks? Here an analogy can help. Consider someone who plays the flute or another wind instrument. Obviously, they need plenty of air in their lungs in order to play, but should not breathe at will – which is why they use so-called breath marks to show them when it is best to do so. A good way to think of punctuation marks is as similar signals to readers, indicating a moment when they can, if they want, draw breath (literally or metaphorically). Cooper (1999, quoted in Mautner 2019: 178) may – deliberately – add a touch too much drama. But her tongue-in cheek advice nonetheless reflects a fundamental truth about punctuation.

> Your sentences shouldn't leave your reader hyperventilating from the constant shallow breaths that over-punctuation requires. Nor should they be gasping for breath at the end of a long, unpunctuated sentence. (Consider yourself responsible for your readers' cardiovascular health.) (n. pag.)

Of course, even the best punctuation can't compensate for badly organised and poorly expressed ideas, just as perfect seasoning cannot make a mediocre dish into a great one. What it can do is to bring out the very best in the chef's creation (or take the edge off it with an excess of salt or a lack of pepper). In fact, seasoning is probably doing its job best when the diner notices neither its presence nor its absence. Much the same is true of punctuation. The purpose of this chapter is thus to help you punctuate unobtrusively yet effectively.[1]

4.1 Why punctuation matters

Punctuation matters because, if done poorly, it can make sentences – and thus whole paragraphs and texts – hard to decode or even downright misleading. A badly punctuated sentence leaves the reader confused or irritated – or both. On the other hand, a well punctuated one makes the reader's life easier because it shows them, among other things, which parts belong together and where they can pause to take a breath.

So it is clear that punctuation isn't merely a formality; it has a real impact on substance and readability. "[W]hen skilfully deployed", guidance on a university's website points out, punctuation "provides you with considerable control over meaning and tone".[2] In fact, there are even wider stylistic implications. Peck and Coyle (2012: 67) argue that "good punctuation can make your work sound weightier and more sophisticated" – surely an important goal in academic writing.

In this book, we present punctuation essentially as an aid to the reader, enabling him or her to divide up paragraphs and sentences in such a way as to maximise readability. It is true that punctuation is partly governed

---

1   If you need or would like more detail than is provided here, the best sources are the online *Chicago Manual of Style* and the style guide of the American Psychological Association (2020).

2   University of Toronto, *Writing Advice*. https://advice.writing.utoronto.ca/revising/punctuation/, accessed 4 June 2022

by grammatical structures, but above all it reflects meaning, rhythm and even the writer's personal style. In this, English differs markedly from other languages, such as German, which offer much less flexibility.

From the writer's point of view, of course, the focus on readability and flexibility is a much more demanding approach than reliance on a strict set of rules. As Siepmann and his co-authors remind us (2022: 222), it means that punctuation – like other aspects of language – involves choices: choices that are not so much between the correct and the incorrect but between the more and the less effective. This approach, incidentally, also means that not even expert writers will necessarily agree on what is good punctuation, so you will inevitably come across advice that differs from ours. Choosing who to follow is another matter for your judgement.

However, once you have become accustomed to it, you'll find that the 'reader support' view of punctuation not only comes to seem natural. It also produces significantly better, smoothly flowing texts that are easy and pleasurable to read. And, what is more, you'll be able to develop your own punctuation style to suit your writing 'personality'. Some writers are 'heavy punctuators'; in case of doubt, they err on the side of caution and provide readers with that extra little piece of guidance. Others are 'light punctuators' and prefer to avoid the risk of becoming intrusive. But both can be *good* punctuators – as long as they are prepared to think about why and how they punctuate.

4.2 What punctuation marks signal

The general principles of punctuation in English we have discussed so far are concerned with the structure of texts, specifically of the sentences that make them up. However, not all the signs that are usually described as punctuation marks are concerned with structural issues. Some indicate that a letter has been left out (as in *isn't* or *it's*) or signal grammatical functions (as in the possessive *Smith's book* or *the studies' findings*). Others are used to identify word-for-word quotations or to express ironic distancing ('scare quotes'). In what follows, we will ignore all these marks and focus solely on those that provide readers with guidance on sentence structure.

The remaining punctuation marks, those we are concerned with here, all mimic a feature of spoken language: regular breaks, of varying duration, in the flow of language. Like the breath marks to the flautist, these punctuation marks suggest to the reader when to draw a (metaphorical) breath – that is, take a break from reading. As a leading authority on academic writing (American Psychological Association 2020) puts it:

> Punctuation establishes the cadence of a sentence, telling the reader where to pause (comma, semicolon, and colon), stop (period [i.e., full stop] and question mark), or take a detour (dash, parentheses, and brackets). Punctuation of a sentence usually denotes a pause in thought; different kinds of punctuation indicate different kinds and lengths of pauses (p. 81).

So when would you, as the writer, want your readers to draw breath? In fact, it is easier to say when you certainly do *not* want them to do so: in the middle of any group of words that they must process together in order to (easily) understand the intended meaning. In the terminology used by Siepmann et al (2022: 223-224), you should not breach the "principle of semantic unity". On the other hand, there are various reasons why you might wish to suggest a brief break:

- To encourage readers to reflect briefly on the previous passage of text;
- To draw particular attention to the previous passage and/or the passage about to start;
- To anticipate the danger of the reader making an inappropriate pause because they are overwhelmed by an upcoming lengthy or more complex passage.

How the pause is to be indicated depends on its desired length and nature. In the remainder of this section, we will examine the various relevant punctuation marks, using the APA's three-part classification into stops, detours, and pauses.

4.2.1 Suggesting 'stops'

We will begin by examining what the APA refers to as "stops", which appear not within sentences but between them. Unless they occur at the end of a paragraph, the two sentences they separate are related to the same 'main idea'. But, by using a stop, the writer is indicating that the ideas and information contained in the first are sufficiently complete in themselves as to warrant brief reflection before the second sentence is tackled. Technically, such stops include exclamation marks, which indicate an instruction or strong emphasis. However, in academic writing they are effectively taboo, associated as they are with over-dramatization, for instance in many advertisements or sensationalist journalism. We will therefore ignore them here.

The ordinary full stop is the punctuation mark that is closest to being rule-determined since it is placed at the end of a complete grammatical sentence. But the rules governing what constitutes a sentence can be broken for rhetorical effect, and writers sometimes place a full stop at the end of what is technically only a phrase or fragment. Like this one, for instance.

The final punctuation mark in this category is the question mark, which is obligatory at the end of direct questions (e.g., *Why has this dimension been ignored so far?*) but is not used after indirect ones (e.g., *We sought to explain why this dimension had previously been ignored.*). That is because its main function is to indicate the rising intonation typical of questions in English, which is not used in indirect questions. Question marks appear a good deal in British academic writing – probably more often than researchers from other academic cultures might expect – in order to provide some variety among the succession of statements and to highlight the point made in the question. Hence their use in the titles of whole articles and their sections (see 1.2.2) and the topic sentences of paragraphs (see 2.2.1). Another reason why the question mark appears fairly frequently is that direct questions can be used to organise texts and to establish immediate rapport with the reader.

4.2.2 Suggesting 'detours'

Next we come to what the APA describes as "detours". These are indications that a part of a sentence is in some sense outside the linear argument of the sentence as a whole.

The dash
The first punctuation mark indicative of such a detour is the dash (–). This is distinguished typographically from hyphens, which separate the elements of a compound word (as in *a fifty-page report; the anti-fascist movement; a decision-making body*). Not only are dashes longer, they have traditionally also been preceded (and, in mid-sentence followed) by a space. However, some publishers prefer to leave no space either before or after a dash.

One common use of dashes is in pairs. In this case, they demarcate some sort of brief comment inserted into a sentence which is not essential to the sentence's overall message, but which the writer nevertheless wishes to call attention to, as in Extract 4.1.

A PAIR OF DASHES INDICATING AN INTERJECTED COMMENT
Extract 4.1 [Elliott & Olive 2021: 109]
It is noticeable that the top four plays are those which were the topic of
A.C. Bradley's Shakespearean Tragedy (1904). We do not suggest that
teachers are directed by a critic who wrote more than a century ago, but
this may point to a convergence – a participation in Muñoz-Valdivieso's
"imagined community" (2017, 76) perhaps – in beliefs about the plays
most worthy of study.

If the comment or other material between the dashes is at all lengthy, there
is a real danger that it may distract from the main line of argument, and a
re-write should be considered.
    The second use of a dash – a single one this time – is to mark off a comment
of some sort at the end of a sentence. On occasion, this is done in order to
indicate a reservation about the earlier part of the sentence. More usually,
though, the dash will precede some sort of climax, often of a surprising
or quirky nature, to which it lends extra emphasis. The two situations are
illustrated in Extracts 4.2 and 4.3, respectively.

A SINGLE DASH BEFORE THE END PART OF A SENTENCE
Extract 4.2 [Chambers & Berger-Walliser 2021: 642][3]
[T]he U.S. legal system is uniquely positioned to provide an effective
forum for victims of corporate human rights violations to pursue their
claims. In the interest of victims, but also to level the playing field for
corporations, and to vindicate its role as a global political leader, it is
time for the United States to reclaim this role – **without the judicial
overreach inherent in some of the previous ATS claims**.

Extract 4.3 [Raw 2021: 1151]
Although it is not usual to find quite so many women together in the
pardon rolls, these examples are useful because they can provide a
control for other, more taciturn sources – **reminding us that absence
of evidence is not evidence of absence**.

---

3   The Alien Tort Statute (ATS) is a U.S. federal law first adopted in 1789 that gives the
     federal courts jurisdiction to hear lawsuits filed by non-U.S. citizens for torts committed
     in violation of international law (https://cja.org/what-we-do/litigation/legal-strategy/t
     he-alien-tort-statute/).

If this second type of dash is used too frequently, it inevitably loses its particular force. Before inserting one, it is therefore advisable to consider whether one of the pause markers discussed in Section 4.2.3 might not actually be more appropriate.

Brackets

Brackets (the round kind known in the US as *parentheses*[4]) also come in pairs and again enclose a piece of information that is not essential in order to understand the sentence in which they appear. (Occasionally, as here, brackets separate off one or more entire sentences, in which case the final full stop precedes the closing bracket.) Unlike dashes, however, brackets suggest no emphasis. They may include a qualification as a means of avoiding a full relative clause, as in this example.

> **BRACKETS USED TO AVOID A RELATIVE CLAUSE**
> **Extract 4.4** [Clegg et. al. 2021: 5]
> O'Neill (2020, p. 16) wrote that 'Companies need a greater purpose, for their own sake as well as societies' because 'As I discovered when leading the independent review into antimicrobial resistance in 2014–15, many market failures are exacerbated by business believing they must purely focus on achieving **(often short-term)** profit targets and ignore societal challenges they can help solve.'

In other cases, brackets contain brief explanations (Extract 4.5) or examples (Extract 4.6) that are usually indicated by the abbreviations *i.e.* and *e.g.*, respectively.

> **BRACKETS CONTAINING EXPLANATIONS AND EXAMPLES**
> **Extract 4.5** [Sanson & Courpasson 2022: 1700][5]
> Other participants than PCI shift-workers **(i.e., retired shift-workers, daily employees and external workers)** and shift-workers from other units were also interviewed to compare perspectives.

---

4   What in America are called *brackets* look like this [...] and are known in the UK as *square brackets*. Their uses in academic writing vary widely, and we will not discuss them here.

5   PCI stands for *Plan Centrale Incendie*, which is the name of a unit within the company discussed in the article.

Extract 4.6 [Beyes & Holt 2020: 17]
In poetic spatial thinking the hierarchy is dissolved, for the object **(the street sign, the atmosphere of domestic calm, the tireless chirr of machinery, the bustle of urban sites)** acquires its status precisely in refusing to be known 'as' something, in refusing subjectification.

As the second example illustrates, however, the abbreviations *i.e.* and *e.g.* may also be omitted. When they do appear, both are usually followed by commas, again as in Extract 4.5. It is also the case that the two abbreviations are generally used only *inside* brackets. *Outside* brackets, they should be replaced with the full forms. Instead of *e.g.*, use *for example, for instance* or *such as*; instead of *i.e.*, use *that is* or *in other words*.

4.2.3 Suggesting 'pauses'

The APA's final group of punctuation marks indicate a more intimate connection between the elements they separate than the stops discussed in Section 4.2.1. The breaks in reading they invite are thus shorter. The shortest of all is indicated by the comma, discussion of which we will postpone until Section 4.3. First, we will examine the two longer 'pauses', indicated by the colon and the semi-colon.

The colon
There is no denying that usage of the colon (:) varies widely in writing generally. We would argue that this situation is unfair to readers as it gives them no clear idea of what a writer is trying to signal with a particular colon. Of course, none of us can come up with 'rules' of colon usage and expect them to be followed universally. But you can at least use colons consistently in your own writing, so that in the course of an article your readers develop a feeling for what you are signalling each time one appears.

Our own suggestion is to use a colon to separate off the end part (or sometimes the beginning) of a sentence. That has several consequences. First, it means there cannot be more than one colon in a single sentence, which after all can have only one 'end' (or beginning). Second, once that 'end part' is complete, the preceding part cannot be picked up and continued – the end must really be the end. And, third, the part of the sentence separated by a colon cannot leave any 'unfinished business' such as a list that is continued in the next sentence. These problems, and possible solutions to them, are illustrated in Makeover 4.1 below.

MAKEOVER 4.1: APPROPRIATE COLON USAGE

Before	*After*
1a. The economy was afflicted by stagflation: that is, a combination of conditions previously thought to be mutually exclusive: high inflation and low, or zero growth.	1b. The economy was afflicted by stagflation, a combination of conditions previously thought to be mutually exclusive: high inflation and low, or zero growth.
2a. We opted for a commonly used approach: corpus analysis, which proved to be highly suitable for the purpose.	2b. We opted for corpus analysis, a commonly used approach that proved to be highly suitable for the purpose.
3a. Some punctuation marks indicate a pause rather longer than that suggested by a comma: brackets and dashes. The colon and semi-colon also fall into this category.	3b. Some punctuation marks indicate a pause rather longer than that suggested by a comma: brackets and dashes, as well as the colon and semi-colon.

Over and above that, we would recommend that the part of a sentence following (or preceding) a colon should not be an entire sentence, as otherwise there is no clear distinction from a semi-colon. However, there are two exceptions to this guidance. One, as discussed in Chapter 6, is that of a longer quotation, the other that of a direct question, as in Extract 4.7. Especially in American usage, the question may begin with a capital letter.

COLON PRECEDING A DIRECT QUESTION
Extract 4.7 [Fu & Cooper 2021: 443]
One important question that naturally follows is: What factors influence nonprofit network portfolios?

Other than in these special cases, the 'end part' separated off by a colon can take various forms. It may be a list, as in the next two examples.

COLON SIGNALLING A PAIR OR LONGER LIST
Extract 4.8 [Alvesson & Sköldberg 2009: 9]
Reflective research, as we define it, has two basic characteristics: careful interpretation and reflection.

Extract 4.9 [Winchenbach, Hanna & Miller 2022: 5]
Four themes developed from the data: 'Reconstructing physical and mental health', 'Navigating customer interactions', 'Feeling valued through community recognition and support' and 'Challenges in constructing the self'.

In these examples, the list items are separated by commas. As we will note shortly, that may also be done by semi-colons, particularly if the items are longer and/or more complex. Alternatively, the items may be bulleted (see 2.2.2).

In other cases, the colon may demarcate a specification of what went immediately before, as in the first example below, or an expansion on the earlier part of the sentence, as in the second.

COLON SIGNALLING A SPECIFICATION OR AN EXPANSION
Extract 4.10 [Bailey 2021: 218]
The distinction between shrine and empty tomb made by William of Malmesbury and John of Beverley's hagiographers has some relevance for the public veneration of another English saint in the twelfth century: that of St Æbbe of Coldingham.

Extract 4.11 [Howarth & Quaglia 2021: 1558]
Our starting point is the incompleteness of the institutional framework of EMU: namely, the uneven degree of centralization assigned to the 'monetary' and 'economic' (notably, fiscal policy) elements (Dyson, 2000; Verdun, 1996).

Finally, the colon may signal an explanation. If that takes the form of a paraphrase, it will be introduced by *in other words, that is* or similar. (Some writers prefer a comma in such cases, but the pause required by the reader before any introductory phrase is clearly longer than the one required after it.)

The semi-colon

The semi-colon (;) is stronger than the comma (i.e., it suggests a slightly longer pause) but weaker than the full stop. Its main function is to combine two complete sentences into a single one without using any linker, and without suggesting the stronger separation associated with a full stop. Thus it is typically used between two sentences whose meanings are closely related, as in Extract 4.12.

SEMI-COLON JOINING TWO CLOSELY RELATED SENTENCES
Extract 4.12 [Jenkins & Delbridge 2020: 14][6]
However, the pressure to meet CHT targets meant that workers often curtailed their impulse to help address and resolve customers' inquiries; the emphasis was on shortening the call rather than dealing effectively with the customer inquiry.

In addition, semi-colons may be used to separate the items of a list if these are longer or more complex, or themselves include commas, as in Extract 4.13.

SEMI-COLONS SEPARATING LIST ITEMS
Extract 4.13 [Howarth & Quaglia 2021: 1565][7]
To summarize, the following measures were adopted to deal with the Covid-related macroeconomic crisis: the de facto suspension of the Stability and Growth Pact (i.e., EU fiscal rules); expansion of ESM lending, with the creation of a specific credit line with significantly lowered conditionality; establishment of SURE to provide loans to member states; and additional EIB guarantees to encourage lending to SMEs.

---

6   *CHT = call handling-time*
7   *ESM = European Stability Mechanism: SURE = European Capacity for Stabilising Employment and Incomes in the Pandemic; EIB = European Investment Bank; SMEs = small and medium-sized enterprises.*

Shorter and less complex items are generally separated by commas, as in Extract 4.9 above.

4.3 Commas: sometimes a question of style

At last, we come to the punctuation mark which is by far the most common of all and indicates the briefest of pauses: the comma. The best way to begin our discussion of its usage is to return to the general principles outlined in Section 4.1. So, to remind ourselves: will readers be assisted in understanding a sentence if they pause momentarily at a particular point, or won't they? (If a momentary pause will be insufficient to do that, then some 'stronger' punctuation mark is required.) Precisely because the pause proposed is so short, the decision whether or not to include a comma is a rather delicate one. We will divide our discussion of the issues involved into two parts: in the first, we will consider those situations in which the decision is pretty clear-cut; in the second, we will examine the grey area where it isn't.[8]

4.3.1 Where style plays little part

In this subsection we will describe a number of situations where a comma is almost always appropriate or almost never appropriate (a summary table is included at the end of the subsection). But please note that we have qualified both statements with *almost*; for, even in these cases, there is often scope – or indeed need – for the writer's judgment.

Where a comma is (almost) never appropriate

Arguably, the greatest problem about comma usage is recognising where a comma is not just unnecessary but actually inappropriate. The first point to be made here is that verbs are never separated from their subjects or objects by a comma. This principle applies even when the subject (or object) is long and complex, a situation which seems to tempt some writers into inserting a comma. The temptation should be resisted. If it arises, it may well be an

---

8   For a more comprehensive guide, see American Psychological Association (2020: 83-84) or the online *Chicago Manual of Style*. If you read German, then Mautner and Ross (2021: 304-309) is another possible source.

indication that the entire sentence needs rewriting to give it a less complex subject and so bring the main verb closer to the sentence start.

The next situation where a writer may be tempted to insert an inappropriate comma, or commas, is that of so-called *defining relative clauses* (see 3.1.3). In Extract 4.14, for example, the clause beginning with *which* defines exactly the *part of the common law* that is meant. Extract 4.15 actually contains two such clauses: the first, starting with *that*, defines the type of *racial and national stereotypes* the sentence will discuss; the second (*which …*) defines the type of *conspiracies* to which such *stereotypes* have *given way*.

'DEFINING' RELATIVE CLAUSE: NO COMMA
Extract 4.14 [McKeown 2021: 225]
The rationale of a decision forms part of the common law **which** binds other courts as well as individuals within the jurisdiction.

Extract 4.15 [Parker 2018: 180-181]
The racial and national stereotypes **that** are used to characterize the villains in the early books give way to conspiracies **which** involve corporations, organized crimes, and terrorists.

Keeping the finger from the comma key when faced with a defining relative clause is likely to be a particular problem for speakers of languages in which *all* relative clauses are delimited by commas. If in doubt, reading the passage concerned aloud and noting whether or not you pause slightly can be a good guide.

The same principle applies to participle clauses (see 3.1.3) where these serve a defining function. The clause that starts with *employing* in Extract 4.16, for instance, tells the reader exactly which *related research* is being discussed.

'DEFINING' PARTICIPLE CLAUSE: NO COMMA
Extract 4.16 [Jarvis, Marsden & Atakav 2020: 91]
As with related research **employing** similar methodology, we make no claim here to the statistical representativeness or generalisability of our findings (e.g. Jackson and Hall, 2016; Jarvis and Lister, 2013).

Extract 4.17 [González-Peño, Franco & Coterón 2021: 8]
In line with the literature and the finding **discussed** above, the results showed an inverse relationship between controlling behavior and student engagement levels.

Another situation that can easily invite an injudicious comma occurs before an object clause (see 3.1.3). Here too, a comma is inappropriate, as illustrated in these two examples.

OBJECT CLAUSE: NO COMMA
Extract 4.18 [Yates & Hartley 2021: 563]
Some argue **that** political astuteness can be acquired (Ferris et al. 2002; Silvester and Wyatt 2018; Doldor 2017) but there is a paucity of information about how this happens.

Extract 4.19 [Wight & Cooper 2022: 1]
We ask **whether** binge-watching can be understood through the existing frames of Cultural Studies, or **whether** the economies of attention, commodification, privatization and surveillance require a different form of critical reflection upon this contemporary practice.

Where a comma is (almost) always appropriate

The first type of 'compulsory' comma is to be found before and, should the sentence continue, after non-defining relative clauses and participle clauses which fulfil the same function (see 3.1.3). In Extract 4.20, *which* refers to *Beverley Minster*, a name that uniquely identifies the building in question, and the relative clause merely provides additional information about it.

COMMAS DELIMITING 'NON-DEFINING' RELATIVE CLAUSES
Extract 4.20 [Bailey 2021: 216]
His cult at Beverley Minster, **which** possessed the saint's relics, was promoted by Bede in the eighth century, and posthumous miracles were credited to him for the next 700 years.[80]

Extract 4.21 [Byng 2019: 244]
The poor, **who** stood or sat in common pews, could not, of course, form a similar kind of bond to their place.

Similarly, the second part of Extract 4.21 refers to all the poor people in the area concerned, and not merely some of them.

This type of relative clause is perhaps not as common in English as some learners seem to suppose. It is therefore well worth considering alternative structures. An obvious choice would often be a participle clause – which would then also have to be delimited by commas. The next two examples illustrate such comma usage, the first before an *-ing* participle clause and the second before an *-ed* participle one.

COMMAS DELIMITING A 'NON-DEFINING' PARTICIPLE CLAUSE

Extract 4.22 [Sanscartier 2020: 50]
These authors illustrate the oft-necessary practice of making ad hoc adjustments to research design, **adapting** to challenges and diversities presented by research contexts and objects.

Extract 4.23 [Lipson 2013: 275]
Both cultures also exhibited a strong sense of racial superiority, **reinforced** by Darwinism; the scientific eugenics work of the period fed into the belief in the superiority of the white race.

A closely related situation is that of so-called appositions. These are phrases that refer to a preceding noun or noun phrase in a different way. Appositions, too, must be demarcated by commas.

COMMAS DELIMITING AN APPOSITION

Extract 4.24 [Renz, Carrington & Badger 2018: 827]
Triangulation, **a term derived from mathematics**, is a method used in research to strengthen the design to increase the ability to interpret findings (Denzin, 1970; Thurmond, 2001) through the use of multiple data sources.

The next juncture where a comma is generally required occurs when an adverbial clause (see 3.1.3) precedes the sentence's main clause, as in the next three extracts.

COMMA FOLLOWING AN INITIAL ADVERBIAL CLAUSE

Extract 4.25 [Chambers & Berger-Walliser 2021: 598]
As the following sections will show, courts and legislators in the United States, Europe, and Canada have overcome these impediments in different ways and to different degrees.

Extract 4.26 [Guess 2021: 1015]
Whereas the overlapping coefficients calculated for 2015 are all well above the somewhat arbitrary 0.5 threshold I identified as

a baseline, the analogous statistics for 2016 do not always meet this standard.

Extract 4.27 [Gross 2022: 449]
To understand the political potentials of the moment, we need to consider what COVID has done to the material conditions of imagination.

In the second extract, note the absence of a comma before *I identified as a baseline*, a defining relative clause (from which the relative pronoun – *that* or *which* – has been omitted).

Introductory participle clauses are treated in exactly the same way as adverbial ones.

COMMA FOLLOWING AN INITIAL PARTICIPLE CLAUSE
Extract 4.28 [Haldane & Turrell 2019: 60]
Drawing on the last seven decades of simulation, macroeconomic agent-based models are one approach with promise.

Extract 4.29 [McLean 2021: 475]
Understood from a different angle, the position of such groups is one of biological essentialism; humans are born with certain sexual characteristics which can never be changed.

Incidentally, Extract 4.29 also provides a good example of semi-colon usage.

The same principle applies even when the element preceding the main clause is not a clause but merely an adverb or an adverbial phrase. The following are examples of the two cases.

COMMAS FOLLOWING AN INITIAL ADVERB OR ADVERBIAL PHRASE
Extract 4.30 [Collinson 2020: 6]
Importantly, Foucault also highlighted the dialectical relationship between power and resistance.

Extract 4.31 [Maitlis & Christianson 2014: 94]
Traditionally, sensemaking has been seen as a retrospective activity, one that can occur only as one looks back over action that has already taken place.

Extract 4.32 [Caserta & Madsen 2019: 4]
Until recently, the confrontation between big law firms and large consultancy companies has been the key conflict for the legal profession.

Extract 4.33 [Heblich, Redding & Sturm 2020: 2063]
In 1801, London's built-up area housed around 1 million people and spanned only 5 miles east to west.

Extract 4.34 [du Plessis 2021: 1]
In Scotland, this matter has been settled definitely through precedent.

Initial linkers that connect the sentence in question to the previous one also fall into this category, as is illustrated twice in Extract 4.35.

COMMAS FOLLOWING INITIAL LINKERS
Extract 4.35 [Jenkins & Delbridge 2020: 5]
However, both empirical testing of these relations and scrutiny of contexts in real-world organizational settings are under-developed. **In addition,** the focus on typifying ethical climates and corrupt organizations limits a more comprehensive assessment of the varied motivations for lying in organizations.

Finally, commas are almost always used to delimit detours in cases where dashes or brackets would be inappropriate. Such insertions may take a variety of forms that are illustrated in the following examples:

- a linker that points backwards in the text;
- a comment;
- a phrase relating to a quotation or citation.

COMMAS DELIMITING BRIEF INSERTIONS
Extract 4.36 [Jarvis, Marsden & Atakav 2020: 94]
Such reflection on difference, **however**, was rarely explicitly celebratory.

Extract 4.37 [Parker & Thomas 2011: 425]
The point is that *Organization*, **probably like the rest of the critical journals we listed above**, is inevitably shaped by its context.

Extract 4.38 [Gaim, Clegg & Cunha 2021: 960][9]
Engines based on the promise of 'clean diesel' were billed as safe for
the environment when in fact, **according to US EPA**, they were on
average 40 times dirtier than US standards (EPA-US, 2015).

Extract 4.39 [Maye-Banbury 2021: 45]
Based on a cursory glance, Charles' newly acquired sunglasses were
suggestive of a cosmopolitan lifestyle which epitomised, **as Brown
(2015) has observed**, being 'cool'.

An exception to this last 'rule' is the conjunction *therefore* (and sometimes
also *thus*), which tends not to be commaed off in mid-sentence, as illustrated
in Extract 4.40.

MID-SENTENCE *THEREFORE* WITHOUT COMMAS
Extract 4.40 [Piekkari, Welch & Westney 2022: 9]
Holistic ethnography **therefore** makes use of the strengths of the
ethnographic tradition to relate the part to the whole.

In Brief
PRINCIPLES OF COMMA USAGE

- **Do not** use a comma in these situations:
    - Before defining relative clauses
    - Before participle clauses with a defining function
    - Before clauses beginning with *that* or *whether*
- **Do** use a comma in these situations:
    - Around non-defining relative or participle clauses
    - Around appositions
    - Following an initial subordinate clause
    - Following an initial adverb, adverbial phrase or linker
    - Around insertions of various sorts

---

9   *EPA = Environmental Protection Agency*

4.3.2 Where style comes in

Between the two extremes of – virtually – always inappropriate and always appropriate, there lie a myriad of cases where a comma may or may not be used depending on the circumstances and the writer's personal judgement. This is where you can develop your own particular punctuation style, be it 'heavy', or 'light' or somewhere in the middle. In this section we will point out some of the most typical situations where a comma is optional and some of the factors that will influence your decisions.

Before we do that, however, we can make a general comment about this zone of opportunity. The principles indicating where to insert a comma may be overridden whenever the sentence itself is (very) short, so that a pause is likely to be intrusive rather than helpful. The following (hypothetical) two-sentence statement illustrates the point. *At first glance, our results strongly support that view. On reflection they do not.* In the first sentence, the pause suggested by the comment emphasises what follows. In the second, on the other hand, a comma would definitely reduce impact.

The Oxford comma

Probably the biggest and best-known debate in this area surrounds the so-called Oxford comma. The term refers to the practice, especially common in American English, of inserting a comma before the *and* that precedes the last item in a list. Extract 4.41 provides an illustration.

> THE OXFORD COMMA IN USE
> **Extract 4.41** [Cheng & Peterson 2021: 159]
> School choice programs and other interventions or public policies may need to pay greater attention to ensuring that families possess the requisite forms of capital – human, economic, **social, and cultural** – to realize their intended benefits.

Yet many writers – in particular those writing in British English – do not automatically insert a comma in this situation, as can be seen in this extract.

THE OXFORD COMMA DISDAINED
Extract 4.42 [Shaw & Bailey 2009: 413]
Discourse analysis is the study of social life, understood through analysis of language in its widest sense (including face-to-face talk, non-verbal interaction, images, **symbols and documents**).[1]

However, that does not mean that opponents of the Oxford comma *never* insert a comma before the final list item. Far from it: they will do so whenever a comma is needed to avoid leading readers 'up the garden path' (i.e., to the wrong interpretation) by failing to clearly separate semantic units (see 4.1) or by leading readers to separate such units incorrectly. In Extract 4.43, for example, the comma after *self-control* cuts off the 'garden path' that would result from interpreting *experience* as a noun.

OXFORD COMMAS CLEARLY SEPARATING THE LAST TWO LIST ITEMS
Extract 4.43 [Ellis et al. 2011: 70]
Feelings of regret and even self-disgust may be strong whenever consumers do not exercise sufficient self-control**, and experience** a bad outcome from their excessive consumption such as a hangover or indigestion.

Extract 4.44 [Llewellyn & Whittle 2019: 836]
Studies have assessed the relevance of behavioural cues such as camouflaged smiling, reduced head movement, increased hand movements, increases in **pitch**, and **speech affectations** (Fielder and Walka, 1993).

Similarly, if there were no comma after *pitch* in Extract 4.44, the reader might be led to think – incorrectly – that the sentence is talking about increases in *both* pitch *and* speech affectations. More generally, if the final list item itself contains an *and*, it should always be preceded by a comma (e.g., *marketing, production, and research and development*).

Adverbial clauses following the main clause
Another situation where style comes into play arises when an adverbial clause starting with a conjunction (e.g., *when, if, although* or *because*) follows the main clause rather than preceding it. The general tendency, particularly in the US, is not to use a comma in this case.

No comma before an adverbial clause
Extract 4.45 [Porter, Shakespeare & Stockl 2021: 639]
In this context, both parties frequently engage in tasks that require harmonious personalities and value preferences. Personal trouble often occurs **when such tasks prompt discordant personalities and values to become visible and to conflict.**

Nonetheless, the 'reading aloud' test suggested above in connection with relative clauses can sometimes suggest that a comma would actually be a good idea. This tends to happen when the adverbial clause begins with a contrastive linker such as *although* or *whereas*, especially when the 'listening' ears are British ones. And, in general, the longer or more complex the adverbial clause, the more likely it is to be preceded by a comma.

A comma before an adverbial clause
Extract 4.46 [Bailey 2021: 208]
The blurring of these two meanings in academic writing has important implications for the present study, **because** it leads to some confusion as to where pilgrims were physically located according to miracle accounts.

In Extract 4.46, for instance, the adverbial clause beginning with *because* itself contains a further subordinate clause: the one starting with *where*. In such cases, the comma is a form of precaution designed to prevent the reader from 'running out of breath' before the end of the sentence – and so from pausing at an inappropriate point.

The 'fanboys' and the broad view
One area where there is considerable variation in comma usage surrounds the seven conjunctions known by the acronym 'fanboys' (*for, and, nor, but, or, yet, so*). These can be used to join two complete sentences (whatever the punctuation mark used between them). Admittedly, fanboys can be found followed by a comma. However, the 'reading aloud' test suggests that a pause is misleading rather than helpful, and we would therefore advise against a comma (see Extract 4.47).

No comma after a fanboy linker

Extract 4.47 [Scales 2022: 337]
Coins establish their trustworthiness as a medium of exchange through their regular, stereotypical appearance. [...] **Yet** coins also function as what Michael Billig, writing about modern societies, has termed 'unwaved flags' of collective identity, [...].[84] ,

Of course, this advice does not apply if the fanboy is followed by an insertion or subordinate clause, as it is in Extracts 4.48 and 4.49.

Comma after a fanboy but before insertion etc.

Extract 4.48 [Byng 2019: 249]
Property owners had a renewed sense of the opportunities, and imperatives, inherent in architectural display, domestic and ecclesiastical, **and, in this,** church and house were linked venues.

Extract 4.49 [Parker 2018: 186]
Bond's gender and ethnicity are even more troubling for "a character who was a cardboard throwback even in the 1960s [...]" (Penny, 2015, p. 31; see also Sparks, 1996).[10] **Yet, whatever the critics might say and have been saying for half a century,** the potential for magical resolution is still there.

Where a fanboy linker occurs in the middle of a compound sentence, it is generally preceded by a comma (Extract 4.50). The comma may be omitted, however, if another follows shortly thereafter (Extract 4.51).

Comma usage before fanboy in compound sentence

Extract 4.50 [Sofaer et. al. 2021: 1124]
However, the ability to mourn and create personal memory statements was severely curtailed during the period, **so** people had to be more selfreliant in creating memory acts.

Extract 4.51 [Gaim, Clegg & Cunha 2021: 956]
Diesel-powered cars are highly fuel-efficient **but this efficiency,** technically, comes at the cost of higher emissions.

In other words, deciding whether to use a comma often involves considering the sentence as a whole, and not just one particular point within it. That broad view is probably what led the authors of Extract 4.52 to adopt a 'light' solution and refrain from placing a comma after *by the late 1960s*, which would have been the third in that sentence. They presumably saw that inserting one would make the sentence distinctly 'choppy' because it would suggest a third pause before readers got to the sentence subject (*a substantial constituency within the discipline*).

AVOIDING A 'CHOPPY' SENTENCE

Extract 4.52 [Parker & Thomas 2011: 422]
For Sociology itself, though its constituent elements clearly predated any self-consciously critical turn, **by the late 1960s** a substantial constituency within the discipline identified itself as necessarily engaged in a struggle with power on either a macro or micro level.

On the other hand, a 'heavy' punctuator would probably see the broad situation differently. They would note that no pauses are desirable inside the main clause beginning with *a substantial constituency*. Accordingly, they would opt for a 'precautionary' comma after *1960s*, designed to prevent the reader from taking a potentially misleading break later in the sentence. Both the light and heavy solutions are perfectly acceptable.

We would end with a general point. If you are having real problems deciding whether or not a comma is advisable at a particular juncture, you may be asking the wrong question. The problem may not be the comma at all; it may just as well be the type of flaw in the sentence structure which can be corrected only by a complete sentence re-write. Such problems can be avoided in the first place if paying attention to punctuation is seen as an integral part of the writing process, rather than as something tagged on at the end. Just like salt and pepper, punctuation is not only for sprinkling on once the dish is served. It should also be used during the cooking process itself.

Chapter 4: The takeaways

- Good punctuation is extremely important in English research texts for reasons of both substance and readability.
- In large part, English punctuation is determined by meaning rather than grammar, although the two approaches often lead to the same conclusions.
- Punctuation marks signal to readers where best to divide up the sentence while they read it, and where they might take the briefest of breaks from reading.
- The length of breaks indicated by punctuation marks can be classified into three groups: 'stops', 'detours' and 'pauses'.
- 'Stops' or longer breaks are suggested by full stops and question marks.
- 'Detours' from the main flow of information in the sentence (e.g., examples or explanations) are suggested by brackets and dashes, usually in pairs.
- A single dash may be used to separate off and highlight a reservation or key point at the end of a sentence.
- 'Pauses', the shortest kind of break, are suggested by colons, semi-colons or commas.
- Commas suggest the briefest of all pauses, and it is through their usage that a writer's style can come into play.
- In some cases, the decision whether to use a comma is more or less clear-cut, whereas in others it is entirely a question of the individual writer's judgement.

5 *Only connect*: Cohesion

> *Words without thoughts never to heaven go.*
> WILLIAM SHAKESPEARE (1564 – 1616),
> *Hamlet, 1.5.98*

Cohesion and coherence are two closely related, but clearly distinct properties of texts. Coherence lies below the surface, as it were, and describes the way the various ideas in a text are grouped and organised. If that arrangement makes sense to the audience, the text is considered coherent and will be easily understood. If it does not, the text will be hard or even impossible to follow. It is safe to assume that coherence is a universal principle; it is a feature of effective human communication in general, and of language in particular.

Where individual languages differ is in the extent to which writers are expected to make use of cohesion: that is, to draw attention on the text's surface to how ideas are connected, for example through linkers such as *because* or *however*. Thus, while coherence is implicit, cohesion is explicit. They are twinned concepts, and well-written texts include their fair share of both.

Compared to many other languages, English makes extensive use of cohesive devices. Indeed, if a typical English academic text were translated directly into, say, Spanish, the result would probably strike its new readership as rather redundant and even patronising. Conversely, if speakers of Spanish and many other languages wish to write effectively in English, they must be prepared to introduce considerably more cohesion into their texts than is likely to come naturally. This chapter will suggest a number of ways in which this can be done, so that your readers are guided through the argument with ease (see also 7.1).

5.1 General principles of cohesion and coherence

The first and most basic principle is that cohesion must reflect coherence. Cohesive devices cannot create coherence where none exists. Merely writing *as a result* at the start of a sentence doesn't make the idea it expresses a consequence of the one set out immediately before. The purpose of cohesive devices is not to establish connections between unconnected ideas, but to point out those connections that, thanks to the text's arrangement, already exist. Again, readers' needs are paramount. If there is underlying coherence but little surface cohesion, they will struggle because they have to work out too much for themselves. If, on the other hand, there are plenty of cohesive devices but no underlying connections to match, then coherence is merely "faked" (Bizup & Williams 2014: 87). In that case, too, readers are short-changed – this time because they may have been tricked into thinking that ideas are related, only to discover that they are not.

Second comes the 'proximity principle': the simplest way of connecting two ideas is to place them close together. The point is illustrated in the following sentence: *Our results suggest a relationship between inflation and individuals' satisfaction with their personal financial situation, which is hard to measure precisely.* Here, proximity will suggest that the *which*-clause refers to *their personal financial situation.* But what if the writer wanted that clause to refer to the *relationship*? In that case, they will have to move the *which*-clause right next to that word: *Our results suggest a relationship, which is hard to measure precisely, between inflation and individuals' satisfaction with their personal financial situation.* Such issues are fairly common in English because a relative pronoun like *which* is not marked for gender and number (i.e., singular or plural) and could therefore refer to any noun, to a phrase or to a complete clause.

The third general principle of cohesion is that of given-new information flow. As discussed in Chapter 3, this states that sentences (and, by extension, paragraphs and other subdivisions of a text) begin with information that the writer expects to be familiar to readers, either because it is part of their general world or subject knowledge, or because it has already been provided in the text. If there is no such flow, then readers will find it hard to establish the connections intended by the writer, and he or she will need to clarify these (see 7.1) – or perhaps rethink the paragraph structure as a whole.

Fourth and last, although we have stressed the relatively high importance of cohesion in English writing, to quote Kipling "there's measure in all things made".[1] Or, as we would more likely say nowadays, *don't go over the top.* Even English readers don't expect or want to have every single connection thrust in their face, and certainly not in the same way every time. Just as in other aspects of (academic) writing we have discussed, variety is essential. Thankfully, cohesive devices can take a number of very different forms, some of which we will discuss in more detail in the next two sections.

In Brief
THE FOUR BASIC PRINCIPLES OF COHESION AND COHERENCE

- Cohesion must reflect coherence.
- Cohesion derives in good part from proximity.
- Cohesion requires consistent given-new information flow.
- Cohesion should make use of a variety of devices so that it does not become intrusive.

5.2 Cohesion within paragraphs

Cohesive devices are not only varied in nature, but also operate at a number of different levels ranging from the individual word, through the syntax of clauses and sentences, right up to ways in which entire paragraphs

---

1   From the short story collection entitled *Rewards and Fairies: King Henry VII and the Shipwrights.*

and indeed whole texts are connected. This last aspect will be dealt with in Section 5.3. For the moment, we will look at the ways in which the connections within individual paragraphs are made explicit, beginning with the role played by words and phrases.

5.2.1 Semantic chains

We have already seen (in 2.2.1) how the topic sentence of an English paragraph, itself a fundamental cohesive device, will typically contain several words of central importance for the main idea to be developed in it. Here, we will examine how such keywords tend to appear repeatedly throughout the remainder of the paragraph. To do so, let us return to our earlier example of a topic sentence (Extract 2.4) and consider in full the paragraph it begins. As you may recall, the keywords concerned are *social, identification, people* and *personally*.

> LEXICAL COHESION
> **Extract 5.1** [Sytch & Kim 2021: 181]
> For **social identification** effects to operate, **people** do not need to know each other **personally**. **Social identification** can emanate from an **asynchronous social** affiliation between **actors**, such as attending the same educational **institution** at **different times**. Although an **interpersonal** relationship can boost the level of **social identification**, the primary factor that triggers **social identification** is **actors'** belonging to the same **social** category. In other words, **people** can claim common **identification** through their shared **institutional** membership even when **personal** connections are absent.

Reading on, we see that these same keywords permeate the entire paragraph; all of them are either repeated, or echoed in some other way, on multiple occasions. The most prominent of all is *identification*, clearly a core technical term in this context, which occurs in each of the paragraph's four sentences. What is more, within that short space it is joined by no less than five synonyms or related words: *affiliation, belonging, relationship, membership* and *connections*. Meanwhile, *social* appears six times (four times in *social identification*, and once each in *social affiliation* and *social category*). And the last two keywords, themselves closely related, are subsequently echoed by members of the same word family: *personally, interpersonal* and *personal.*

Known as *semantic chains,* such strings of words and their close associates play a key cohesive role. Though they often begin in a paragraph's topic sentence, that is not always the case. In Extract 5.1, for instance, *asynchronous* and *institution* in the second sentence are echoed, respectively, by *different times* later in the same sentence and by *institutional* in the last. Semantic chains are fundamental in 'weaving' a text together. Not all paragraphs are as densely woven as this example, it is true. But many good ones are.

In the example above, the various chains are made up only of synonyms and members of the same word family. But that need not be the case. Other semantic relations can play a role, too. Thus chains may include:

- antonyms (i.e., opposites) such as *human* and *animal/non-human*;
- umbrella terms and their subcategories (e.g., *disciplines* incorporating *economics* and *linguistics*, say);
- names of wholes and their constituent parts (e.g., *Europe* versus *Portugal, France, Poland* etc.).

Repetition: good or bad?

The semantic chains we have identified show how important it is in cohesive terms to repeat words and concepts verbatim (i.e., word for word). Repetition makes sure that readers understand the message as easily as possible. It allows them to see how every sentence emerges from those before it and leads on to those that follow. Given that, it is rather puzzling that the technique is often seen as a problem. True, repetition can be bad, and sometimes very bad, when it is not necessary and comes across as intrusive. But it can also be good, when it contributes to the precise transmission of meaning.

What matters is the kind of words being repeated. Those that are technical terms in a specific context (i.e., have a precise technical definition in the field concerned) can be repeated without hesitation. In fact, they *must* be repeated in the name of clarity, precision and consistency – principles which, in academic writing, are ultimately more important than aesthetic criteria. In Extract 5.1 above, for example, this definitely applies to *(social) identification.* It could be replaced only if another term were generally accepted among scholars in the field as an exact synonym: that is, as having not only the same basic meaning but also the same connotations.

Where repetition really ought to be avoided, on the other hand, is in the area of more general vocabulary. There it is likely to give the impression that the writer's command of English is not all it might be, as well as making the text boring. For instance, the authors of Extract 5.1 could have chosen to repeat the word *emanate*. By instead reformulating the idea in question with a different verb (*trigger*), they make the passage more interesting to read.

Similar considerations apply to Extract 5.2. Here, too, technical terms are repeated assiduously, both alone and in various combinations: *Brexit, anti-establishment, politics* (along with *political* and *politically*), *alienation* (and *alienated*). What might appear to be tempting synonyms – *alternative* for *anti-establishment, disengagement* for *alienation, the UK's departure from Europe* for *Brexit* – are systematically ignored, and quite rightly so.

REPETITION OF TECHNICAL TERMS
Extract 5.2 [Fox 2021: 16]
A common interpretation of the UK's **Brexit** vote is that it was an expression of **anti-establishment** sentiment, outrage and dismay from a **politically alienated** majority. This line of thinking suggests **Brexit**, like the electoral appeal of Donald Trump and parties such as the Five Star Movement, is but the latest manifestation of a growing disconnect between Western citizens and their democratic institutions. The direct role of political **alienation** in building support for such **anti-establishment** causes has, however, barely been examined. This study addresses this gap and uses previous literature on political **alienation** to build a model to test the claim that **Brexit** was (at least in part) driven by **political alienation** in UK citizens. The analyses show that while **political alienation** did have a substantial effect in making some citizens more likely to support **Brexit** – specifically those who lacked trust in the integrity of the **political** elite and felt that the **political** system was unresponsive – its impact overall was limited. Moreover, claims that **Brexit** was driven by **political alienation** understate how **alienated** from politics most people who were opposed to it also feel.

General vocabulary, however, is not repeated; *impact* avoids repetition of *effect; sentiment* in the first sentence leaves the door open for *feel* in the last; *examined* does the same for *study*. *Claim* is indeed repeated, but arguably it constitutes a technical term in this type of research discourse. *Citizens* on the other hand, seems to be a genuine borderline case in this example; repeated three times, it is replaced in the final sentence with *people*.

Such borderline cases are not uncommon, because the difference between technical and general vocabulary is not as clear-cut as popular accounts of language would often have us believe. Far from being an inherent quality possessed by individual words in isolation, as such accounts suggest, a word's 'technicality' depends on the field under discussion and the terminology, or jargon, common in that. For example, it would never occur to most people that *happiness* might be considered a technical term. Yet in the growing discipline of happiness studies that is exactly what it is – and thus eminently repeatable.

5.2.2 Pronouns

Pronouns are words that stand in for, or accompany nouns (or even whole clauses). Examples include *she, this, which, the former, their* and *theirs*. Pronouns can therefore be used cohesively, especially to avoid intrusive repetition in cases where nouns lack appropriate synonyms. Yet using pronouns, as opposed to repeating the noun to which they refer (known as their *referent*), inevitably opens up the possibility of misunderstanding. Given the need for absolute clarity in academic texts, pronouns must be used with more care than in texts generally.

Nonetheless, they still have an important part to play in establishing cohesion, as is illustrated in Extract 5.3 (in this example and the next, only those pronouns with a cohesive function inside the paragraph are highlighted).

COHESIVE USE OF PRONOUNS (#1)
Extract 5.3 [Guess 2021: 1008]
Additionally, some worry that hidden algorithms could speed along this process by replicating and reinforcing people's preferences on social media without **their** awareness (Pariser 2011). **This** is exemplified by frequent lamentations in the popular press about the ideological cocooning of America via social media (e.g., Klasa 2016; Madrigal 2017). **These** concerns evidently resonate with the mass public: People generally believe that consulting like-minded sources for election news

is common, especially among **their** political opponents (Perryman 2017).

This passage contains three cohesive pronouns: *their*, which twice refers back to *people*; *this*, whose referent is the entire clause *some worry [...] their awareness*; and *these*, which strengthens the lexical link between *concerns* and its synonym *lamentations*.

Extract 5.4 includes two similar instances of *their* (the referents being, respectively, *boundaries* and *volunteers*) and one of *these*, which here strengthens the lexical link between *boundaries* and *scripts of belonging*. It also features *them* (i.e., *the scripts for belonging*), *themselves* (*refugees*) and – three times – *they* (*these boundaries*), as well as the relative pronoun *which* (*hierarchies*).

COHESIVE USE OF PRONOUNS (#2)
Extract 5.4 [Wall 2021: 5101]
While boundaries may be established by those with the most power, even those with seemingly little power may participate in **their** creation and/or policing. For example, even in the case of volunteers offering assistance to refugees, **their** actions establish boundaries and hierarchies in **which** hospitality is often conditional and informed by formal and informal rules (Kyriakidou, 2020). Likewise, refugees themselves may internalize the scripts for belonging and then use **them** to police fellow newcomers or even **themselves** (Murray, 2014). However, it is important to note that **these** boundaries are rarely impenetrable and may be challenged, disrupted, or reworked (Yuval-Davis, Wemyss, & Cassidy, 2018). **They** can be fluid and can change depending on relationships and the passage of time; **they** can be in a constant state of becoming as **they** are produced and coproduced (Frazer, 2020).

Pronouns are very common and usually paid little attention. However, using them is a good deal more challenging than many writers realise. For, if there is any doubt whatsoever about what a particular pronoun refers to, readers may be confused – or even misinterpret the passage concerned. In the *Before* version of Makeover 5.1, we have highlighted five pronouns with unclear referents and inserted after each of them an indication of the candidates for this role.

MAKEOVER 5.1: AVOIDING AMBIGUOUS PRONOUNS

Before

The 1979 referendum on Scottish devolution was singularly ill-timed from **its** [*the referendum* or *devolution?*] supporters' perspective. On the one hand, devolution's main backer, the Scottish National Party, had recently seen its run of electoral successes halted by two by-election defeats. **They** [*defeats* or *successes* or *the SNP?*] were accordingly in a state of turmoil at the time of the crucial poll, **which** [*the poll* or *a state of turmoil?*] was both cause and effect of internal tension. On the other hand, the referendum came at the tail-end of a severe winter. **This** [*the winter* or *the timing of the referendum?*] greatly reduced the chances of the high turnout essential if **it** [*high turnout* or *the severe winter* or *something else?*] was to receive the votes of 40% of all Scots eligible to vote and thus satisfy a condition imposed by the UK parliament.
[Paragraph from a fictional paper designed for publication in a Scottish political journal]

After

Seen from the perspective of those who supported Scottish devolution, the 1979 referendum on the subject was singularly ill-timed. On the one hand, devolution's main backer, the Scottish National Party (SNP), had recently seen its run of electoral successes halted by two by-election defeats. At the time of the crucial poll, the party was thus in a state of turmoil that was both cause and effect of internal tension. On the other hand, the referendum was held at the tail-end of a severe winter. This circumstance greatly reduced the chances of the high turnout needed to ensure that support for devolution would exceed the 40% of all Scots eligible to vote, as required by the UK parliament.

These issues are resolved in the *After* paragraph by various techniques, as follows:

- Replacing the pronoun *its* with its referent *Scottish devolution*;
- Replacing the pronoun *they* with a synonym (*the party*) of its referent: *the SNP*;
- Placing the relative pronoun *that* immediately after its referent *a state of turmoil*;

- Replacing the pronoun *this* with a noun phrase (*this circumstance*) which refers back to the previous sentence in its entirety;
- Replacing the pronoun *it* with its referent *devolution.*

To conclude this subsection, we should mention one pronoun and one 'pseudo-pronoun': that is, a word that can function as if it were a pronoun. The pronoun proper is *such (a)*, which is widely used in front of nouns, as in Extract 5.5, to indicate 'things (here *expectations*) of this type'.

TYPICAL USE OF *SUCH* AS A PRONOUN
Extract 5.5 [MacDowell 2018: 268-269]
Furthermore, the way she is shown perkily prancing towards the physical closet might suggest we are about to experience the familiar sight of a 90s comic Hollywood heroine playfully perusing a rack of outfits (perhaps in a pop-driven montage). **Such** expectations having been conjured, the revelation of the computer screen establishes we are instead dealing with a character who regards selecting clothes in this peculiarly impersonal manner to be equally commonplace as the more routine activities we were encouraged to anticipate.

The 'pseudo-pronoun' is the definite article *the*, which often has a cohesive function similar to that of a pronoun. In Extract 5.6, for instance, both *the outlet* and *the site* refer to the website mentioned in the paragraph's first sentence.

***THE* IN A COHESIVE ROLE**
Extract 5.6 [Neff 2022: 6-7]
Non-commercial funding enables Carbon Brief to work at a different pace than its commercial colleagues and produce coverage such as long-form analyses and fact-checks that may break from traditional forms of journalism. **The outlet** also seeks to be an authoritative source of climate science and policy information for journalists. [...]. **The site**'s staff pays attention, often via Twitter, to conversations that journalists have around environmental issues and may get involved if they see, for example, a journalist being led into conversations with those peddling dubious science, or vice versa.

5.2.3 Linkers

A third way of creating cohesion is by means of linking expressions like *because*, *however* and *by contrast*. Such linkers can connect individual words or phrases, but here we will focus on their use to connect clauses or sentences. It is important to note that they are not merely 'fillers'. Far from it: they are explicit pointers to relationships which readers would otherwise have to work out for themselves. Quite simply, linkers make the reader's life easier. Having said that, the general principle of not overdoing cohesion applies especially to linkers. Used excessively, they can become annoying and appear rather patronising. They are therefore to be used discerningly and in as great a variety as possible.

The next example shows neatly how a selection of well-chosen linkers (highlighted in bold) can work together to establish various types of connection and so make the argument flow smoothly.

EFFECTIVE LINKER USAGE
Extract 5.7 [Butler & Spoelstra 2020: 416]
However, in this article we are interested less in philosophical theories of metaphor than in the sociological analysis of metaphors-in-use. **Even if** we accept that language is ultimately metaphorical, it is **also** true that people (ourselves included) use metaphors in daily life **as if** there were a clear distinction between the figurative and the literal. Quite apart from any philosophical objections, metaphors practically help us to make sense of the world around us and communicate what we see and experience. We are **therefore** interested in what social actors achieve by drawing on such rhetorical tropes and how figurative language influences organizational behavior – in our case, how critical scholars relate to their own work.

This example works particularly well because the four linkers employed to establish cohesion within the paragraph are well dispersed, all different and indicate four different types of connection.[2] The functions of the linkers used in this text, as well as other common ones, are explained in Toolbox 5.1.

Three remarks are in order about *therefore*, which is used impeccably in Extract 5.7 but often both over- and misused. First, a note on spelling: the final *e* cannot be left out. There is an English word *therefor* (without *e*), but it has a

---

2   The initial *however* is, of course, also a linker, but the connection it establishes is with the previous paragraph, not within the one shown.

totally different meaning and is virtually never used today. Second, *therefore* is used typically in the middle of sentences rather than at their beginning, and then without the commas that generally accompany other linkers in that position (see 4.3.1). And, third, like all other linkers indicating a cause or reason, it must be used only when there is a genuinely causal relation. If the relation is vaguer and more general, other options must be considered (e.g., *thus*).

Toolbox 5.1
COMMON LINKERS, WHAT THEY INDICATE & WHAT THEY JOIN

Indicating	Joining	Linkers
Cause/reason	Clauses	*as; because; since*
	Sentences	*that is because*
	Both	*for*
Result/effect	Sentences	*as a result; consequently; accordingly*
	Both	*so*
Addition to list	Sentences	*in addition; furthermore; moreover*
	Both	*(both) ... and; (neither) ... nor*
Alternative	Sentences	*alternatively; instead; on the other hand*
	Both	*(either) ... or*
Generalisation	Both	*generally; on the whole; by and large*
Specification	Both	*specifically; in particular; indeed*
Similarity	Clauses	*just as*
	Sentences	*similarly; likewise*
Difference	Clauses	*whereas; while*
	Sentences	*by/in contrast; in/by comparison; on the other hand*
Concession	Clauses	*although; even if; even though*
	Sentences	*admittedly; it is true (that); of course*
Response to concession	Sentences	*however; nevertheless; nonetheless*
	Both	*but; yet*
Summary	Sentences	*in brief; in sum; to recap; to sum up*

To close our discussion of linkers, we should mention a particular type that could be described as *concessive*. Their function is illustrated in Extract 5.8.

A CONCESSIVE LINKER

Extract 5.8 [Warner, Houle & Kaiser 2021: 205]

Although disadvantaged groups may carry lower absolute debt than more advantaged populations, they have higher debt burdens relative to their economic resources (e.g., debt to income [DTI]) and more difficulty repaying these debts (Tach and Greene 2014).

The initial *although*-clause 'concedes' that *disadvantaged groups* actually fare better than *advantaged groups* in one respect. But, as *although* has already primed the reader to expect, the following main clause presents two points that outweigh the concession, thus confirming that the former groups really are disadvantaged. Other linkers that perform the same function as *although* are *even though, though* and *even if.*

The weakness of these concessive linkers is that they work only within the confines of a single sentence, which must include both the concession and the subsequent overriding argument. This effectively restricts their use to short, relatively simple concessions. Where concessions are more complex, or several are to be made with regard to the same point, writers can make use of a so-called 'Yes, but' structure (see 7.2.1). In this case, the concession(s) is/are introduced by a linker such as *admittedly* or *it is true (that)*, while the overriding argument begins with another linker, such as *but* or *however*, and – here lies the structure's attraction – can be placed in a separate sentence.

In Toolbox 5.1, we have set out some of the linkers that are most common in academic writing, together with the type of connection they indicate and the elements they can be used to join (clauses, sentences or both). Of course, the list is by no means exhaustive, not least because linkers do not constitute a clearly defined grammatical category. For that same reason, they are not usually covered systematically in grammar books aimed at non-linguists.[3]

---

3   A good deal of useful information can be found on the *Cambridge Dictionary* website: https://dictionary.cambridge.org/grammar/british-grammar/conjunctions-and-linking-words. Those who read German will find a more detailed and structured account in Mautner & Ross (2021), Chapter 20.

In Brief
USING LINKERS

- Linkers are far more than 'fillers'; they are crucial in clarifying connections for readers.
- They work best if they are used in great variety and not too often.
- Like all cohesive devices, they can only reflect underlying connections that already exist, not create new ones out of thin air.
- In particular, they can be used to indicate concessions.

5.2.4 Structural devices

In the discussion of Makeover 5.1, you may have noticed that, while pronoun ambiguities can often be resolved by using different words, they are sometimes best dealt with by changing sentence structures. However, the importance of structure in establishing cohesion extends well beyond that. In the following we will examine some of its other uses.

Parallel grammatical structures

First, the connections between sets of statements can be strengthened by giving them the same grammatical pattern. For instance, successive sentences may be phrased as questions, begin with the same phrase or take the form of cleft-sentences (see 7.2.2). Whatever the pattern repeated, this technique will work best if the sentences concerned are kept short. It is illustrated in Makeover 5.2.

MAKEOVER 5.2:
IMPROVING COHESION AND IMPACT THROUGH PARALLEL STRUCTURES

Before

After

1a. Having established exactly what happened during the 1990 disturbances, we must now consider the reasons behind these events and the impact they had on the country's subsequent development.

1b. We have now established exactly what happened during the 1990 disturbances. But what were the reasons behind these events? And what impact did they have on the country's subsequent development?

2a. The business faces three problems. First, the firm is currently unable to raise sufficient funds. Second, it has recently lost three senior management figures in swift succession. And, third, the company is facing difficulties in attracting good staff.

2b. The business faces three problems. It cannot currently raise sufficient funds. It cannot easily attract good staff. And it cannot retain those it has, having recently lost three senior management figures in swift succession.

3a. Medical professionals must provide the scientific input on which health policies are based. However, deciding on the policies should be left to politicians. And policy implementation will largely be a matter for individual citizens.

3b. It is medical professionals who must provide the scientific input to health policy making. But it is politicians who must decide on the policies. And, to a large extent, it will be individual citizens who implement their decisions.

Advance organisers

Another widely-used structural device is the so-called *advance organiser*. This gives readers a preview of the structure and/or content of the immediately following passage, as in this example.

AN ADVANCE ORGANISER PRECEDING A LIST

Extract 5.9 [Chambers & Berger-Walliser 2021: 584-585][4]

The problem presented to courts and policy makers around the globe **is twofold. First,** what is the legal basis for human rights victims' claims against corporations that, in one way or another, contribute to, or are complicit in, human rights violations committed by other private or governmental entities? **Second**, where should plaintiffs be allowed to bring such claims – before the courts of the country where the human rights violation took place, the courts of the MNC's home state, or even in a third country's jurisdiction?

In Extract 5.9, *twofold* in the first sentence indicates that a list containing two items is coming up, thus avoiding the need for rather clumsy linking phrases (such as *a second problem facing courts and policy makers is the following*). Cohesion is then further strengthened by the use of the listing linkers *first* and *second,* and by the parallel question structures.

In Brief
COHESIVE DEVICES WITHIN PARAGRAPHS

- **Lexical cohesion** created by semantic chains of related words and by repeating technical terms in the field concerned
- **Pronouns**, with particular care being required to ensure that it is absolutely clear what they refer to
- **Linkers,** used in moderation and wide variety
- **Structural devices**, in particular parallel sentence structures and advance organisers

---

4   *MNC = multinational corporation*

5.3 Cohesion beyond the paragraph

Just as sentences must be joined up to form paragraphs, so must paragraphs be connected to form texts. The underlying principles remain the same, but implementing them presents additional challenges. For, in the nature of things, proximity now plays less of a role in establishing cohesion – especially if paragraphs are on the long side – although it remains an important factor, in particular at the boundaries between paragraphs. As a result, cohesive devices (i.e., semantic relationships and syntactic connectors) must be made to work between elements that are sometimes separated by considerable amounts of text.

The divide represented by the paragraph boundary also has to be bridged. As we indicated in Section 2.1, moving from one paragraph to the next involves a switch to a new topic or, at the least, to a new aspect of the same topic. As a result, the opportunity for establishing semantic chains that straddle the boundary may be reduced. And if there is a complete change of topic, that opportunity may effectively vanish. But many of the other devices used to establish cohesion within paragraphs are equally useful at the inter-paragraph level, although they may need to be more numerous and/or stronger (i.e., more explicit).

Linkers
Most obviously, entire paragraphs may be connected by linkers. The three extracts below provide typical examples.

> LINKERS ESTABLISHING INTER-PARAGRAPH COHESION
> **Extract 5.10** [Spence 2021: 4]
> If this turns out to be true, it means that the share of income going to capital will grow. If the ownership of capital is concentrated, there is clearly a problem of rising income inequality looming.
>
> **In addition**, under the trend of industry digitization, only those firms that adopt bold strategies and conduct disruptive innovation will survive in the rat race. [...]
>
> **Extract 5.11** [Thomas 2021: 703]
> Grue (2016, p. 840) argues that while the argument has been made that "a positive depiction of people with impairment is a good thing in itself," some "ostensibly positive portrayals of marginalised and oppressed groups and individuals contribute to marginalisation and oppression." [...]

Similarly, Darke (2004) critiques ostensibly positive depictions in the media which remain, for him, clichéd and stereotypical. [...]

Extract 5.12 [Butler & Spoelstra 2020: 416]
This metaphor connects two fields of meaning – that is, academic work (the topic) and game-playing (the vehicle) – by revealing the "partial resemblance" of one to the other.

Of course, there are philosophical objections to the concept of metaphor. [...]

However, in this article we are interested less in philosophical theories of metaphor than in the sociological analysis of metaphors-in-use.

The connections established in the three examples are all different in nature. In the first one, *in addition* is used to connect two paragraphs, each of which discusses a consequence of developments in AI. Other linkers that can serve the same listing function at the inter-paragraph level include *first, second*, etc., *furthermore* or *moreover* and, to indicate the last paragraph in the list, *finally*. In Extract 5.11, the inter-paragraph link established is one of similarity. In Extract 5.12, on the other hand, a concessive linker (see 7.2.1) at the start of one paragraph paves the way for the *however* that occupies the same position in the next.

Advance organisers

Advance organisers are another device that can be used beyond the individual paragraph, albeit in a different form. A particular case here is that of a text's introduction (or the introduction to a long section). As we pointed out earlier, that usually ends with an orientation paragraph (see 1.2.2) laying out for the reader what will be coming up in the text as a whole.

More generally, a writer will often wish to provide their readers with a similar preview to a series of paragraphs which, taken as a whole, relates to a single overarching idea. Sometimes, the preview is contained within the topic sentence of the first paragraph in the series, as in Extract 5.13.

ADVANCE ORGANISERS AT THE PARAGRAPH LEVEL
Extract 5.13 [Renz, Carrington & Badger 2018: 827]
Four types of triangulation (Denzin, 1978) have been described, including methods triangulation, otherwise known as mixed-methods or multimethods triangulation, where both quantitative and qualitative data are generated. [...]

The other three types of triangulation include investigator triangulation (the use of one or more observer, coder, or data analyst), theoretical triangulation (the use of multiple theories to examine a hypothesis), and data analysis triangulation. [...]

Extract 5.14 [Sofaer et. al. 2021: 1126]
The responses by visitors discussed above reveal the perceived needs that visits to heritage sites can satisfy. In order to further understand the ways in which visitors use heritage sites in support of wellbeing it is useful to employ **the concepts of hedonic (subjective) and eudaimonic (psychological) wellbeing**.
Hedonic wellbeing [subheading]
[...]
Eudaimonic wellbeing [subheading]
[...]

On other occasions the preview will be given a separate orientation paragraph of its own, as in Extract 5.14 (note how, as pointed out in Section 2.1, paragraphs of this type may infringe the general three-sentence minimum-length rule). In this case, the text's authors have strengthened the cohesive effect even further. First, they have made the two groups of paragraphs that follow the orientation paragraph into separate headed subsections. And second, the headings of these two subdivisions are terms appearing in that paragraph.

Topic sentences

Within a headed section (or subsection), cohesion can be strengthened by ensuring that the topic sentences of individual paragraphs are all related in some way to the section heading. In Extract 5.15, the word *continuum* featured there is echoed by its opposite (*dichotomy*) in the topic sentence of the first paragraph, and by a synonym (*cline*) in the paragraph's concluding sentence.

TOPIC SENTENCES LINKED TO A SECTION HEADING
Extract 5.15 [Hyland 2017: 19-20]
4. A **continuum** of metadiscourse
These different views are often presented as a **dichotomy** between a narrow text-centred view and a broad interpersonal one (e.g. Maur-

anen, 1993). [...] Conceptions of metadiscourse, and individual studies themselves, are more usefully seen as contributing different aspects to our understanding of discourse and as occupying different points on a **cline** rather than two opposed positions.

Of the section's remaining four paragraphs (omitted here for reasons of space), three have topic sentences that include one or other of the two terms: *At one end of the* **continuum** *researchers believe ...; Further along the* **continuum***, we find ...; At the other end of the* **cline***, ...* (And in the fourth, *cline* appears in the second sentence.) In this way a very high level of cohesion is achieved. The example is perhaps a particularly fine one, but the principle it illustrates applies generally.

Moreover, the topic sentences of paragraphs play a key role in establishing cohesion at the juncture between successive paragraphs. In Extract 5.16, for example, the topic sentence of the second paragraph includes the phrase *these two meanings*, which echoes the two passages emboldened in the first paragraph.

TOPIC SENTENCE LINKING TWO PARAGRAPHS (#1)
Extract 5.16 [Bailey 2021: 208; see also Extract 4.46]
The task of trying to understand pilgrims' experiences in high medieval England is not helped by a conceptual problem concerning the word 'shrine' in modern academic usage. **It has become commonplace to use the term as a synonym for 'cult centre'**, broadly referring to a religious institution housing a saint. **However, the word 'shrine' also has a narrower definition.** Derived from the Latin *scrinium* – meaning a container of sacred items – it additionally pertains to a material object: an artefact containing holy relics, usually the corporeal remains of a saint.

The blurring of **these two meanings** in academic writing has important implications for the present study, because it leads to some confusion as to where pilgrims were physically located according to miracle accounts. [...]

The connection established is particularly strong if it links a topic sentence to the final sentence of the paragraph before, as it does in our next example.

TOPIC SENTENCE LINKING TWO PARAGRAPHS (#2)

Extract 5.17 [Chambers & Berger-Walliser 2021: 594]

There is certainly an argument that directly pleading a breach of human rights standards, as opposed to conventional tort liability, would be symbolic and more socially significant to victims. Hence, **the question** of direct horizontal effect of international human rights remains relevant despite the proliferation of conventional tort claims.

The answer will likely depend on the way in which international law affects a country's domestic legal order, and will require further doctrinal refinement. [...]

In Brief
COHESIVE DEVICES BEYOND THE PARAGRAPH

- Linkers, including concessive ones
- Advance organisers, in the form of topic sentences or entire paragraphs
- Topic sentences that:
    - echo the section title
    - include a (lexical) connection to the preceding paragraph

A final word of caution

To conclude, a final remark that relates to all the devices discussed in this section. Assuming individual paragraphs are internally coherent, then linking them in these ways will ensure that the text overall exhibits the "flow and connectivity"[5] that is one of the hallmarks of compelling academic writing. Yet, to recap a point we made in Section 5.1, surface cohesion is not a magic bullet. It won't help if the text is lacking in underlying coherence.

---

5   https://www.sheffield.ac.uk/ssid/301/study-skills/writing/academic-writing/paragrap
     h-flow-connectivity

In fact, should it turn out during the editing process that, however hard you try, you just can't come up with good devices to join up successive paragraphs, then there is every chance that the problem actually runs deeper. Maybe the content of the paragraphs in question is such that they should be in a different order, or perhaps moved to a different section. Or perhaps deleted altogether.

Chapter 5: The takeaways

- Cohesion derives in the first instance from proximity, but must also be established overtly by a range of cohesive devices.
- Within paragraphs, the most commonly used devices are:
    - □ repetition of technical vocabulary (but not of general vocabulary)
    - □ semantic chains of synonyms and other related words
    - □ pronouns, the use of which requires considerable care in order to avoid any ambiguity about what they refer to
    - □ linkers, which should be used adequately but judiciously, and in sufficient variety
    - □ structural devices such as parallelism and advance organisers
- All of these devices, especially linkers and advance organisers, can also contribute to cohesion beyond the paragraph level, as can the topic (and final) sentences of paragraphs.

6 *Your words, not mine*: Citations

> *If I have seen further, it is by standing on*
> *the shoulders of giants.*
> Isaac Newton (1643 – 1727)

Ample use of citations is one of the hallmarks of academic writing. Once written up, even the most innovative research must be linked to earlier work by other researchers (whether true 'giants' or not). You may not agree with them, but they have to be given a voice so that you can engage with their theories, methods and results. Only then can fruitful academic discussion begin, for it is mainly through publications that scholars 'talk' to each other.

Over and above that, there are various legal, ethical and academic reasons why we have to cite sources. Essentially, they boil down to the following.

1. Writers must respect intellectual property rights. Whether or not a country has formally enshrined these rights in law, it is an ethical imperative to give credit where credit is due. Anyone who fails to do so commits theft.
2. Writers need to establish credibility. They must back up their claims and arguments with evidence that readers can follow up, evaluate and critique. For experienced readers, your in-text citations and your references – that is, the list of sources at the end – also add up to a profile of your research, particularly its theoretical and methodological orientation.
3. Writers have to connect to the "scholarly conversations" (Curry & Lillis 2013: 70) that have shaped the field. Even the most groundbreaking discovery will in some way be indebted to the research that preceded it. However radical the departure, these roots must be acknowledged. Writers need to identify clearly where in the relevant research traditions their own contribution is located and what it adds to the "larger narrative" (Hyland 2000: 20), which will also continue into the future.

These three reasons add up to a fourth. If you handle citations competently, you demonstrate that you have mastered an essential tool of the trade. Thus, even though some citation conventions may seem petty and far removed from the world of ideas, accuracy in these matters will also reflect positively on your credentials as a scholar. As Booth et al. (2016: 203) rightly point out, "many experienced researchers think that if a writer can't get the little things right, he [sic] can't be trusted on the big ones".

As an academic practice, citing sources involves a number of issues ranging from the substantive (e.g., what to quote) to the purely mechanical (e.g., how to format references). For the latter, we refer readers to general style guides such as the *APA Publication Manual* and the (online) *Chicago Manual of Style*, as well as to instructions issued by individual publishers, journals, departments and supervisors. At the more substantive level, which we will deal with here, citation practices are linked to fundamental questions about academic integrity and the social, dialogic nature of research.

WHAT'S COMING UP

6.1   What to cite and how much
6.2   Types of citations
      6.2.1   Direct versus indirect citations
      6.2.2   Integral versus non-integral citations
6.3   Weaving citations into the text
6.4   Inadvertent plagiarism and how to avoid it

6.1 What to cite and how much

Before moving on to more detailed citation conventions, we will address four general questions that trainee writers often ask.

What kind of material can I quote?

The first question concerns the nature of sources. What exactly counts as 'quotable' material? No one will have any doubt that academic books and papers in learned journals fall into this category. But what about articles in popular newspapers, lecture notes, blogs and pdfs uploaded to personal websites? And Wikipedia?

In essence, the legitimacy or otherwise of a source depends on what you use it for. Disciplines that work with textual data – literary studies, linguistics and sociology, to name just a few – distinguish between so-called primary and secondary sources. Primary sources are texts that you analyse as data – for example, a play by Molière, an election manifesto, the transcript of a focus group discussing racism in social media, Wikipedia entries on climate change. As primary data, any kind of text is fine (provided it has been obtained legally and there are no ethical or copyright issues).

By contrast, secondary sources are cited because of their scholarly value as the output of research, and the weight they add to your arguments as a result (with both value and weight depending on the quality and status of the publication medium, as well as the reputation of the author). To take just the first of our earlier examples, the corresponding secondary sources would be books, articles and other established academic genres that *deal with* Molière and his works. The reliability and reputation of these sources derive from the multi-layered gatekeeping processes that control their production. There are usually several rounds of revisions based on editors' and reviewers' critical comments. If such quality assurance processes are in place and up to international standards, then the material in question can be used as a secondary source; if they're not, steer well clear of it.

In this context, we should also briefly consider scenarios in which a citation is *not* necessary. We do not have to provide evidence for general knowledge and incontrovertible facts. That Paris is the capital of France; that combustion engines emit CO_2; and that George Washington was the first President of the United States: none of this would have to be backed up by citations. That said, in academia generally and perhaps in the humanities and social sciences in particular, there is a tendency to be very cautious about treating things as 'incontrovertible'. What may seem entirely straightforward and uncontroversial to the average lay person may in fact be steeped in controversy among scholars. If that is the case, then of course these debates must be adequately reflected in your work, and citations are a key vehicle for doing so.

How many citations should I use?

The second question concerns the number of citations. There is no simple answer to that; a great deal depends on the type of publication, the topic, the field, the writer's career stage and confidence, and (up to a point) their personal style. Even the section of the thesis, paper or book plays a role. In the introduction as well as in sections describing the theoretical framework or reviewing the relevant literature, there will be many more citations than in those parts that present the author's own empirical work. In the discussion section, citations often come back in, because this is where findings are interpreted and related back to the context outlined both in the introduction and the lit review. Finally, the closer we get to the conclusion, ready to wrap up our argument, the less we will want to open new lines of argument by engaging with many other voices. Commenting on a book's penultimate paragraph, Hayot (2014: 153) reminds us that this is "not a great place to be throwing around new names, which will send the reader's mind haring off in new directions."

There is an important clue here which goes a long way towards answering the question posed in the heading of this subsection. As so often in English academic writing, it is the readers that should be the centre of attention. They should not be smothered with a blanket patched together with quotations, so that they can no longer make out the underlying fabric of your own contribution. Yet they should be given as many citations as they need to locate your research in the field's ongoing narratives, and to distinguish your voice from that of other writers.

With the reader in mind, you will also find it easier to accept the rationale behind many citation conventions. Page numbers, for example, are essential in helping the reader find a specific passage, though they may be dispensed with when it is the whole article or book that is referred to (see Extract 6.17 for two examples of the latter). You may find it tiresome to follow all the rules for signalling deletions and additions from sources quoted word for word. But they suddenly make sense if you bear in mind the reader's right to see an accurate version of the original (not to mention the right of the quoted author not to be misrepresented).

And what about my own voice in all this?

The third general question is about writers' fear that the voices of the authors they cite may drown out their own. The risk is there, but it can be minimised if citations are handled properly, on the basis of advice we gave earlier in this section and will elaborate further below. We can offer some general guidelines, two of which are brief and straightforward. One is to cite as much as necessary but not more, the other to use word-for-word quotations only when they are essential.

Beyond that, a little more commentary is in order. As we will explain, it is essential to ensure that all citations are suitably integrated into your text. "Since quotations do not speak for themselves", Graff and Birkenstein (2021: 49) explain, "you need to build a frame around them in which you do that speaking for them". This framing is in itself a highly demanding responsibility, but also a privilege that enables you to make your own voice heard. For, however many authors you cite, however large the "choir" of different voices becomes (Siepmann et al. 2022: 49), you remain the choirmaster. It is you, and you alone, that orientates all the different voices towards your personal research story.

Can I re-use my own work, and is that plagiarism?
Strictly speaking, it is not possible to plagiarise your own research – just as you can't steal your own bike. Yet it is not uncommon for copyright to be transferred to the publisher, with the author only retaining *the moral right to be identified as the author*, as the standard phrase from publishing contracts goes. Under such arrangements, you cannot in fact re-use your own material at will, but would have to get the publisher's permission before citing extensively from it.

However, legal questions aside, recycling chunks from your own publications is definitely frowned upon, as numerous contributions to online fora testify. (Try googling *self-plagiarism* and you'll see how this question exercises the academic community.) There is of course nothing wrong with returning to ideas, theories and methods you have worked with and published previously, but you will be expected to recontextualise and rephrase them. What is more, you will also be expected to properly cite your earlier work. This can be done by simply adding a source reference – in parentheses or a footnote – or by making the process explicit in the body of the text (e.g., *as I have argued elsewhere*; *in a previous study my co-authors and I have shown that ...*).

In Brief
PRINCIPLES OF CITATION

- Cite from sources with good gatekeeping practices wherever possible, but any source will do if used to provide *primary* data (copyright laws and ethics codes permitting).
- Cite liberally in the earlier part of a research text, less so as you move towards the conclusion.
- Cite as much as necessary but not more, and use word-for-word quotes only when necessary.
- Frame citations so as to orientate them towards your own work – and thus introduce your own voice into the text.
- Cite yourself sparingly, and preferably only to reappraise or build on earlier ideas of your own.

6.2 Types of citations

In this section, we will be looking at different types of citations, and what the distinctions mean for how the quoted material is framed by the running text. Two basic rules hold true for all types though. One is that every citation must be followed by a source reference. This may appear in a footnote, a practice that has survived in history and the law, for example. Alternatively, it may use the 'author-date' method and be included in parentheses as part of the running text, as illustrated by the extracts in the remainder of this section.

This format, referred to as *parenthetical notation* or *Harvard style refer- encing*, is now the norm in the social sciences and also in many humanities disciplines. Both it and source referencing in footnotes exist in a wide variety of styles, with different rules applying to such matters as the use of punctuation and capital letters. For such specifics, make sure you consult whichever style guide you are obliged to follow.

The second general rule is that you must always find the original source and read the relevant sections yourself before citing them. This rule can be broken, but only under the exceptional – and, given digitalisation, increasingly rare – circumstance that a source really cannot be traced. In that case you add *quoted in* or *(as) cited in* to the source reference for the work you have personally consulted. Rather confusingly, this type of citation is referred to as a *secondary citation*. If both sources involved – the one you've actually seen, and the one you haven't – are printed publications, they must both be included in the reference list.

6.2.1 Direct versus indirect citations

Probably the most important categorisation of citations is the division into direct and indirect quotations. It recognises that an author's intellectual property really consists of two parts: an idea or argument, and the precise way in which that is expressed.

Direct citations
Direct citations are verbatim (i.e., word for word) and so emphasise the quoted author's wording. If they are relatively short (roughly up to three lines), they are placed between quotation marks (either single or double, depending on the publisher's policy) and displayed as part of the run-on text. All these points are illustrated in the next two examples.

TYPICAL SHORT DIRECT CITATIONS

Extract 6.1 [Evans 2020: 881][1]

At one of those meetings, in 1965, microbiologist and later Nobelist Salvador Luria stated that the public should be consulted because for scientists to "claim the right to decide alone" about the direction of scientific efforts would be "to advocate technocracy" (Luria, 1965, p. 3, 17).

Extract 6.2 [Collier & Cox 2021: 291]

Thus, O'Hare et al. (2016, p. 1176) write that the 'ambitions of insurance as a mode of resilience are overwhelmingly stability orientated, rebounding to a preshock "normality" where risk is absorbed by a system, but rarely avoided or reduced'.

As can be seen in Extract 6.2, quoted material inside a citation is placed between the type of quotation marks not used for the citation as a whole (so here, 'double within single').

Longer direct citations are set off as block quotes (i.e., separate paragraphs). These have no quotation marks, but they are indented and they may use a smaller font and narrower line spacing than the body of the text (see Extract 6.3). How and where the source reference is given depends on the relevant style guide.

DIRECT CITATION (LONGER, BLOCKED)

Extract 6.3 [Graham 2018: 189-190]

Habits are socially inculcated and so a Pragmatic ethics is socially focused and grounded in education:

> The moral and the social quality of conduct are, in the last analysis, identical with each other ... the measure of the worth of the administration, curriculum, and methods of instruction of the school is the extent to which they are animated by a social spirit. And the great danger which threatens school work is the absence of conditions which make possible a social spirit. (Dewey, 1916/2008, p. 307)

---

[1]   Note that the full stop at the end of Extract 6.1 follows the source reference rather than preceding it. This is a general rule that applies to all punctuation marks.

Block quotes lend citations additional prominence. Nonetheless, they are generally preceded or followed by a brief summary highlighting their key points. That is certainly an advisable practice, whether or not Hayot (2014: 156) is right to identify what he calls the "dirty secret" of block quotes: "most readers don't actually read them". What his comment does definitely remind us of is that such quotes should be used only if the entire wording, or at least the greatest part of it, is essential to the point the writer wishes to make.

How to use direct citations

As we have mentioned, the rules governing direct citations are very strict. Under no circumstance must the original be changed in any way without indicating explicitly what changes have been made. Grammatical or typographical errors must not be silently corrected, but marked with *sic* (Latin for *so*), usually inside square brackets, as in: "Various applications of this method has [sic] turned out to be successful."

Errors of fact, on the other hand, must be commented on more elaborately (e.g., *Jones incorrectly asserts that* ...). If you have discovered a genuine flaw in another researcher's reasoning, merely adding *sic* will not do. You will be expected to engage properly with the flawed argument, explaining in some detail what its flaws are, and making a case for a correct alternative.

Apart from footnote numbers,[2] nothing may be omitted from a direct citation if doing so might distort the meaning in any way. If you do decide to omit something, then the omission must be indicated. This is done by inserting three ellipsis points (i.e., dots), with or without brackets (again, the relevant style guide will tell you what to do exactly). Extracts 6.5 and 6.6 will provide examples.[3]

Needless to say, you must be very careful that no omission distorts the message. There are obvious no-gos such as omitting *not* or *never*, but in less blatant cases more discretion may be required. You must avoid even slightly misrepresenting an author you quote, for example by omitting words and phrases that qualify a statement (think of adverbials such as *under certain circumstances* or *strangely enough*), or by quoting one half of their argument but not the other. The ellipsis points merely mark a deletion; they cannot

---

2   The *Chicago Manual of Style* says these may be omitted "unless omissions would affect the meaning of the quotation". (See also our remarks in the Explanatory Notes.)

3   In-text references (e.g., *Smith, drawing on Brown, suggests* ...) should never be omitted.

cure a misrepresentation. And when dealing with sources, it is best to err on the side of caution.

Occasionally, it may be necessary to *add* something to a direct quotation. Citations are inevitably lifted out of their original context, so readers may need help interpreting them. It may no longer be clear, for example, who or what pronouns such as *she* or *they* refer to, or what an acronym stands for. The necessary glosses are provided between square brackets. Thus, in a paper discussing a particular play, you might find: "In Act II, she [Jane Smith] appears to have a revelatory experience"; and in another on postcolonialism: "A year later, the SPFS [Society for Francophone Postcolonial Studies] was founded."

If you use italics or bold face to highlight a word or phrase in the quoted passage, you indicate the addition by *emphasis added* or *my emphasis* after a comma and the source reference, as in the next extract. After *my emphasis*, you may add your initials.

SOURCE REFERENCE INDICATING ADDED EMPHASIS
Extract 6.4 [Edgar, Brennan & Power 2021: 30]
However, leaders can use words to "sculpt reality" (Vignone, 2012, p. 35) and an "audience's interpretation of and reaction to a person, event, or discourse can be shaped by the *frame* in which that information is viewed" (Benoit, 2001, p. 72, emphasis added).

Another permitted intervention is to adjust the quotation marks if the passage quoted itself contains some. If your style guide tells you to use double quotation marks for the quotation as a whole, then any double marks within it must be changed to single. Should the guide require single marks for quotations, then any of these that occur inside a quotation must be doubled.

When to use direct citations
Verbatim rendering should be used only if it is either worthwhile or absolutely necessary. It is worthwhile if the original wording is particularly striking and adds rhetorical weight to your own argument (see Extract 6.5).

DIRECT CITATION WITH STRIKING WORDING
Extract 6.5 [Gross 2022: 450]
It has been part of neoliberalism's hegemonic formation to condition everyday life, including both leisure and work, in ways that compress the space of political possibility. David Graeber (2013) describes how neoliberalism has been a project waging 'a relentless campaign against the human imagination. [...] We are talking about the murdering of dreams, the imposition of an apparatus of hopelessness, designed to squelch any sense of an alternative' (p. 281).

A direct citation can be necessary for a number of reasons: for example, if it comes from a text that is itself the object of analysis, as may occur in literary or legal studies.

DIRECT CITATION FROM A LITERARY WORK UNDER ANALYSIS
Extract 6.6 [Banerjee 2020: 133]
Even as Charles Dickens's Little Dorrit (1857) centers on the Marshalsea Prison (indeed, its eponymous character is born in it), the novel invests considerable narrative energy in bringing to life another, albeit fictional, institution: the Circumlocution Office. Ostensibly modeled on the Treasury Office, the Circumlocution Office had "its finger ... in the largest public pie, and in the smallest public tart."[1]

Second, a verbatim quotation is necessary if it includes a term or phrase relevant in its own right, as is *game* in Extract 6.7, which comes from a paper that deconstructs the notion of 'publication game'.

DIRECT CITATION INCLUDING A KEY TERM
Extract 6.7 [Butler & Spoelstra 2020: 414]
Academia is often characterized as a game that involves players and rules. For example, scholars are said to be involved in a "publication game" (Townsend, 2012), a "publish-or-perish game" (Martin, 2014), or a "research game" (Lucas, 2006).

Third, the precise wording of a citation, however unexciting, may be essential because it is a definition, as in the next two examples, or for some other strong reason.

DIRECT CITATIONS INCLUDING A DEFINITION

Extract 6.8 [Mishra 2018: 48]

Article 10(1) of the ECHR states that 'everyone has the right to freedom of expression'[24] and that the right shall include 'freedom to hold opinions and to receive and impart information and ideas without interference by public authority and regardless of frontiers'.[25]

Extract 6.9 [Moore 2018: 2]

This article examines how special artists used flag imagery in illustrations to communicate news about the war as sentiments of nationalism. Proceeding with a definition from Anthony D. Smith, nationalism is understood as "an ideological movement for attaining and maintaining autonomy, unity, and identity for a population which some of its members deem to constitute an actual or potential 'nation.'"[3]

Indirect citations

If none of these reasons for using a direct citation apply, then an indirect one is preferable. Indirect citations focus on *what* an author says rather than *how* he or she says it, and they always appear in the running text. They reproduce another writer's ideas or arguments without using the exact original words and therefore have no quotation marks before or after. The absence of these does not leave the writer open to accusations of plagiarism, since the source reference tells readers unmistakably that the idea or argument is someone else's intellectual property. More than that: readers are reassured that, by going back to the source indicated, they can find the same idea, only expressed in different words.

As can be seen in the following examples, the source reference is not preceded by *see*; this is reserved for cases in which you want to direct the reader to additional literature (which is why we often find phrases such as *see also* or *for further details, see …*).

TYPICAL INDIRECT CITATIONS

Extract 6.10 [Gaim, Clegg & Cunha 2021: 950]

Paradoxes are difficult, costly and precarious to manage effectively (Andriopoulos & Lewis, 2010; Smith, 2014). Not only are they difficult to achieve but they are even harder to maintain over time (Abdallah, Denis, & Langley, 2011).

Extract 6.11 [Fleming 2021: 2]
Post-election cabinet reshuffles are significant political events. Like all cabinet reshuffles, they can have important consequences for prime ministerial influence (Indriðason and Kam, 2008; Kam and Indriðason, 2005), policy outcomes (Alexiadou, 2015), government popularity (Dewan and Dowding, 2005; Miwa, 2018), future election results (Martin, 2016) and parliamentary accountability (Thompson, 2020).

Extract 6.12 [McKeown 2021: 226]
Whilst Adel (2006) sets forth a relatively settled definition and model of reflexive metadiscourse, Adel (2017) represents a more fluid and open-ended approach.

Extract 6.13 [Beyes & Holt 2020: 11]
As Fredric Jameson (1991, pp. 410-12) suggests, the spatial turn has come in the wake of an inexhaustible expansion of capital into increasingly restless, elusive spaces such as cruise tourism, platform-mediated politics or global branding.

To cite indirectly, you have to summarise or paraphrase the original, in a wording noticeably different from it. Genuine paraphrasing does not merely consist in replacing a word or two, changing the punctuation or splitting up a couple of sentences. If this is all you do and 'forget' the quotation marks, you will still have committed plagiarism. Likewise, simply translating a passage from a source does not count as a proper paraphrase either, but merely as "translingual plagiarism" (Siepmann et al. 2022: 49).

One thing best avoided in summarising and paraphrasing is figurative language, such as metaphors, because of the significant risk of implying interpretations incompatible with the quoted author's intentions. Even metaphors used in the orginal are best dispensed with; if they are especially striking, then a direct quotation is called for. In fact, paraphrases generally employ rather bland language. Toolbox 6.1 indicates some standard techniques for generating them.

Toolbox 6.1
PARAPHRASING TECHNIQUES

- **Using synonyms** (e.g., *soared* → *rose sharply*; *imprecise* → *vague*; *slightly* → *minimally*)
- **Changing word class** (e.g., *selection* → *select*; *develop* → *development*; *vague description* → *described vaguely*)
- **Changing sentence structure** (e.g., *Although initial results are promising, it is too early for firm conclusions* → *First results have shown promise, but definitive conclusions would be premature.*)

How might these techniques be applied in practice? Suppose you wish to cite, indirectly, this passage from the conclusion of an article on the British trans-gender movement (McLean 2021: 480).

A determined group of people have taken their cues from fellow-thinkers in the United States to lobby for the GRA [Gender Recognition Act] not to be positively reformed for trans people, but to actively make life more difficult for them by denying them rights they currently enjoy and have been practicing for years.

You might come up with something along these lines.

McLean (2021: 480) concludes that, inspired by similar groups across the Atlantic, some in the UK have been set on depriving trans people of well-established rights and campaigning against pro-trans reforms of the GRA.

This transformation has used all the techniques set out in Toolbox 6.1, as most successful paraphrases will. There are structural changes (the US connection has been moved forward and converted into a participle clause, and the two objectives of the anti-trans campaign have swapped positions); there are word-class changes (*be reformed* → *reforms*); and some synonyms have been introduced (*fellow-thinkers* → *similar groups*; *deny* → *deprive*). Additionally, *determined* has been converted into *set on*, *in the United States* has become *across the Atlantic*, *lobby for … not* is now *campaigned against*, and *rights they currently enjoy and have been practicing for years* is summarised as *well-established rights*. Note, though, that the option of a more evocative, but also more loaded synonym for *fellow-thinkers* (e.g., *co-religionists*) has been rejected in favour of the non-committal *some*.

In Brief
DIRECT AND INDIRECT CITATIONS COMPARED

Direct citations	Indirect citations
■ Emphasise form (i.e., the way an idea or argument is worded in the source)	■ Emphasise content (i.e., the idea or argument expressed in the source)
■ Repeat the exact words used in the source	■ Summarise or paraphrase a passage from the source
■ Have quotation marks around them (unless they are block quotes)	■ Have no quotation marks

But both types must have source references.

6.2.2 Integral versus non-integral citations

A further categorisation of citations is into what Hyland (2000: 22) calls *integral* and *non-integral* types. The distinction between these two citation strategies relates to the way the source reference is presented. In an integral citation, the name or names of the author(s) is/are integrated into the running text, as in these two examples.

INTEGRAL CITATIONS
Extract 6.14 [Jarvis, Marsden & Atakav 2020: 86]
Politicians, as Uberoi and Modood (2010: 303) note, 'seem keen to promote Britishness using the state', irrespective, indeed, of party allegiances.

Extract 6.15 [Goodlad 2021: 110]
In their much-discussed *Empire* (2000), Michael Hardt and Antonio Negri sought to radicalize political action through focus on the possibilities of self-organizing collectivities.

If, on the other hand, the name or names appear only in brackets, as in Extracts 6.16 and 6.17, then the citation is non-integral.

NON-INTEGRAL CITATIONS

Extract 6.16 [Fu & Cooper 2021: 439]
Interorganizational networks describe systems of "high interdependence among otherwise autonomous agencies" (Lawless & Moore, p. 1167).

Extract 6.17 [Daniels 2022: 3]
Critical race theory also stresses the mutability and historical contingency of racialisation, racial projects, and racial formations (Omi and Winant 2002 [1986]; Mullings 2005).

Why should this distinction be of interest to writers? Because it allows them to choose whether they want to foreground or background a cited author's identity. If foregrounded, in an integral citation, that author is given a stronger voice and becomes more visibly part of the case you are building. If backgrounded, in a non-integral citation, readers are allowed to concentrate more on the content of the argument and less on who made it.

In practice, the choice between these two strategies is also influenced by stylistic considerations. Using too many integral citations risks overloading the text with names and drowning out your own voice. Yet it is impossible to say exactly how many is too many. It may depend on 'micro' factors such as how a particular paragraph is structured, or on 'macro' factors such as what is considered standard usage in a discipline. Finding the right balance comes with experience.

Attention and weight accorded to cited authors and their contributions

As you may well have picked up from the examples above, this second categorisation of citations is independent of the first, into direct and indirect types. There are thus four different options, between all of which skilled writers tend to alternate – for the reasons given above but also quite simply in order to ensure stylistic variation. The four options are summarised in Table 6.1.

	Integral citation Author's name appears in the running text	Non-integral citation Author's name appears in brackets or a footnote
Direct citation ■ Verbatim quote ■ Source reference ■ Quotation marks	*... which Lee (2017: 23) calls "odd".* (See also Extract 6.14)	*... which has been called "odd" (Lee 2017: 23).* (See also Extract 6.16)
Indirect citation ■ Paraphrase ■ Source reference ■ No quotation marks	*... which Lee (2017: 23) considers to be unusual.* (See also Extract 6.15)	*... which is considered unusual (Lee 2017: 23).* (See also Extract 6.17)

Table 6.1. The four citation types

If we consider both dimensions simultaneously – direct vs indirect and integral vs non-integral – we can see a spectrum emerging in terms of the attention given to cited authors and the weight attributed to their contributions. At one end of the cline, a verbatim quote combined with in-text mention of the author's name guarantees maximum attention both to the author and to the exact words he or she used. At the other end of the spectrum, a paraphrase with the author's name tucked away in parentheses or a footnote makes the citation much less conspicuous. The other two options lie between these two poles, sharing characteristics of both.

6.3 Weaving citations into the text

Whatever type they may be, citations must be woven seamlessly into the text so as to enhance their message rather than distracting from it. There are two main ways in which this can be achieved. One is to embed the quote in the grammar of the surrounding text, as in Extracts 6.18 and 6.19.

GRAMMATICALLY EMBEDDED CITATIONS
Extract 6.18 [Grossman 2019: 1264]
This expansion of the definition of diaspora caused much confusion, as writers began to use the term indiscriminately, applying it to all kinds

of groups and individuals and turning it into "an all-purpose word" (Faist 2010, 14).

Extract 6.19 [Thomas 2021: 694]
Films and related media have been censured for aligning with a medical/tragedy model of disability (Green & Loseke, 2020) which represents disabled people as "pathetic" (French & Swain, 2004, p. 34), as vulnerable and in need of charity (Goggin, 2009), and as "objects of spectacle" (Norden, 1994, p. 1).

Alternatively, citations may be framed by what are known as *reporting verbs*. The next four extracts provide typical examples.

Citations introduced by reporting verbs
Extract 6.20 [Gaim, Clegg & Cunha 2021: 964-965]
Laufer (2003, p. 257) **argued** that constant pressure on middle and lower management to produce results fosters an environment in which tacit acceptance of illegalities and turning a blind eye to deviance increases their tolerance throughout the hierarchy.

Extract 6.21 [Larue 2020: 4]
Lietaer **claims** that there is a causal link between the diversity and resilience of natural ecosystems, and between their resilience and their stability.

Extract 6.22 [Clegg et al. 2021: 2]
As Cooper (1976, p. 1000) **wrote**, 'given a fixed, specific purpose, everything adjusts itself to that purpose'.

Extract 6.23 [MacDowell 2018: 262]
Perhaps the most sustained and famous critique of interpretation in film studies is David Bordwell's Making Meaning, and it similarly **proposes** that "what may matter as much as [interpreting] implicit or symptomatic meanings is the surface of the work" (1989, p. 264).

A reporting verb inevitably says something about the citation it frames and your attitude towards the quoted material. *Demand* and *insist,* for instance, imply a degree of forcefulness on the quoted author's part. The verb *claim* tends to suggest that the quoting author disagrees with, or disapproves of the quote's content in some way. Any other verbs you may use (without qualifying them as discussed below) are generally taken to imply your broad agreement with the citation, while some make your agreement more or less explicit. Toolbox 6.2 lists common verbs in these two (admittedly fuzzy) categories.

Toolbox 6.2
REPORTING VERBS SUPPORTIVE OF CITATION

Explicit support	*advise; advocate; confirm; emphasise; explain; point out; reaffirm; recommend; show*
Implicit support	*argue; comment; conclude; indicate; note; observe; remark; report; state; suggest; write*

This categorisation is to be treated with care, however. Support can be converted into doubt or mild dissent by the addition of a suitable adverb (see Toolbox 6.3). Outright criticism, on the other hand, is generally packaged more diplomatically (e.g., *our evidence seems to point in the other direction ...*). Even adverbs signalling doubt or mild dissent may be toned down further by a preceding adverb such as *somewhat, slightly* or *perhaps*. Conversely, an adverb can also be used to signal explicit support, as in Extract 6.24.

SUPPORT FOR QUOTED MATERIAL BY MEANS OF AN ADVERB
Extract 6.24 [Shaikh 2022: 65]
Third, Sraffa **correctly** argues, in favor of Marx, that empirical economic aggregates are essentially the same in prices and values.

Toolbox 6.3
ADVERBS INDICATING ATTITUDES TO A CITATION

Endorsement	*rightly; correctly; usefully; helpfully; instructively; revealingly; tellingly*
Doubt / mild dissent	*perhaps questionably; somewhat contentiously; maybe a little misleadingly*

In expressing their stance towards the quoted material – neutral, supportive or doubtful – writers may even introduce themselves into the text by using *I* or *we*, as the case may be.

USE OF *I* TO EXPLICITLY SUPPORT QUOTED MATERIAL

Extract 6.25 [Grossman 2019: 1265]
My conceptualization is more positivist than constructivist in that I view diasporas as actual social formations as well as social constructs. Nonetheless, **I agree** with Sökefeld (2006, 265) that "it is difficult conceptually to separate diaspora as social form from diaspora as a type of consciousness," and **I follow** Sheffer's (2003, 19) recommendation to combine these approaches when researching diasporas. As the remainder of this article shows, I have tried to do this by synthesizing disparate definitions of diaspora.

Returning to reporting verbs themselves, these can appear in the present tense (Extract 6.26), present perfect (Extract 6.27) or past (Extracts 6.28 and 6.29).

TENSE USAGE WITH REPORTING VERBS

Extract 6.26 [Cheng & Peterson 2021: 159]
In a classic study, Wilson (1991:462) **emphasizes** the social isolation of people from different class and racial backgrounds who live in impoverished neighborhoods: They lack quality schools, suitable marriage partners, and adequate "exposure to informal mainstream social networks and conventional role models." He **theorizes** that programs designed to promote equality of opportunity that have positive effects on the moderately disadvantaged may have little or no effect on those he **refers** to as the "truly disadvantaged" (Wilson 2012).

Extract 6.27 [Larue 2020: 1]
Several authors **have** for long **warned** that constant economic growth is leading to the depletion of natural resources and is putting an excessive strain on environmental sustainability (Daly, 1990; Georgescu-Roegen, 1974; Jackson, 2016).

Extract 6.28 [Renz, Carrington & Badger 2018: 827]
Denzin (1970) **suggested** that the use of triangulation has the potential to increase the validity of the study, decrease researcher bias, and provide multiple perspectives of the phenomenon under study.

Extract 6.29 [Edgar, Brennan & Power 2021: 31]
We select Carillion as our case because the UK parliamentary enquiry (House of Commons, 2018a, p. 86) **found** Carillion management's behaviour to be self-serving: "The individuals who failed in their responsibilities, in running Carillion and in challenging, advising or regulating it, were often acting entirely in line with their personal incentives".

One cannot really go wrong with the present tense (unless the sentence includes elements that 'trigger' other tenses). As for the other two options, there are no hard-and-fast rules for choosing between them. Some tendencies can be identified however (Swales & Feak 1994: 182-184). The present perfect tense is often used for general references, or references to more than one source: to *previous research* or *several studies*, for example. Individual publications, by contrast, may be referred to in the past tense (as in 6.28 and 6.29), particularly if they are not recent. (If the reporting verb is in the past tense and the citation is indirect, the rules governing indirect speech should be applied, with tense shift kicking in.[4])

Finally, reporting verbs are not the only way of introducing citations. In the interest of variety, these may also be reported by means of prepositional phrases, as in the first example below.

VERBLESS REPORTING STRUCTURES
Extract 6.30 [Taylor 2020: 177]
In so far as theories and explanations of the special sciences are adequate, **according to** Sider, the categories they feature must be at least reasonably joint-carving (Sider 2011: 22).

Extract 6.31 [Mackin 2022: 783]
In this sense, I agree with Duvenage's (2003) **suggestion that** Habermas should conceive of aesthetic practices and experiences as aspects of communicative experience in general (cf. 2003, 118).

---

4   See Hewings (2013: 32-39) or, if you read German, Mautner and Ross (2021: 120-132).

Alternatively, a noun phrase may be used as in Extract 6.31, where *suggests* has become *suggestion*.

6.4 Inadvertent plagiarism and how to avoid it

Plagiarism is primarily associated with an intention to deceive for personal gain. However, as Turabian (2018: 81) reminds us, "inadvertent plagiarism" is also possible. It has two common causes: misunderstandings about the rules of direct and indirect citation, on the one hand, and sloppy research practice on the other. So how can one guard against it? We have dealt with this question intermittently throughout this chapter. However, the issues involved are so important and potentially serious that we are picking them up again here. Drawing on Turabian (2018: 81-83), Toolbox 6.4 offers hands-on advice on how to avoid plagiarising 'by accident'.

Toolbox 6.4
AVOIDING INADVERTENT PLAGIARISM

- Insert source references *whenever* you draw on other people's work, whether it is by:
  - quoting word-for-word what they have written
  - summarising or paraphrasing their ideas and arguments
  - using a theory or method that they have developed
- Make sure that verbatim quotations are:
  - signalled by quotation marks or set off as a block quote
  - worded exactly as they were in the source, down to the smallest detail
- Double-check that your summaries and paraphrases of sources do *not* use the original wording.

Knowing these rules and being willing to apply them is necessary, but not sufficient. You also need to critically examine and carefully organise your research routines, especially the way you read, take notes and save material on your computer – because it is in this area that plagiarism is most likely to happen accidentally. "The most common problem", Booth et al. (2016: 207) explain, "is not that students don't know that they should cite a source, but that they lose track of which words are theirs and which are borrowed".

For example, you might come across an interesting passage in a journal article published online, copy a paragraph or two into a Word file full of your own notes, but forget to add the quotation marks and the source reference. Initially, you will probably have no difficulty remembering where these two paragraphs came from, and that they are not in fact your own intellectual property. Returning to the same file months later, however, you could well have forgotten what came from where, and the paragraphs written by someone else may have merged imperceptibly with text written by yourself. You then write up your thesis or paper using all the notes from that file without realising that some of them are actually stolen goods. And, with plagiarism, lack of intent is not an acceptable defence.

To prevent such errors, it is essential to develop a note-taking and writing routine which, from the very start of each project, recognises the need for detailed and robust documentation. Sound project management, of course, also helps because it reduces time pressure, increasing the scope to check and double-check your citations while reducing the temptation to cut corners.

Chapter 6: The takeaways

- Only sources with good gatekeeping practices should be cited as secondary sources, but any may be used for primary data collection (provided that legal and ethical requirements are met).
- Citations should be used sufficiently but not needlessly. Introduce your own voice by framing them appropriately.
- Direct (i.e., verbatim) citations:
  □ appear as part of the running text inside quotation marks or blocked without quotation marks
  □ are used only when the original wording (not just the idea) is important for some reason
- Indirect citations (without quotation marks) are used when there is no cause for a direct one.
- All citations, whether direct or indirect, must be followed by a precise source reference.
- In integral citations, the quoted author's name is included in the running text; in non-integral ones it appears only within the source reference.
- Citations must be woven into the running text by:
  □ embedding them in its grammatical structure
  □ using reporting verbs
- The support for a citation's content can be weakened or intensified by means of adverbs.
- Not only intentional but also inadvertent plagiarism is taboo. When noting down any material obtained from any source, always record the source reference exactly, including the relevant page number(s), and place quotation marks around any verbatim wordings.

7 *Follow me*:
Guiding and persuading the reader

I can't write without a reader. It's precisely
like a kiss – you can't do it alone.
JOHN CHEEVER (1912 – 1982)

Our final pillar is one that may not be immediately associated with academic texts: the means to nudge readers towards acceptance of the writer's case. This may seem at odds with the notion that academic language ought to be 'objective'. Yet, although not completely unfounded, that demand ignores the fundamentally persuasive nature of academic writing. As Sword (2012) explains:

> Academic writers often strive to convey a completely neutral perspective; as merchants of truth rather than fiction, we see it as our job to inform our readers, not to play with their expectations or their minds. Yet that neutrality turns out to be something of a myth. All academics are partisans, after all, arguing for the validity of our theories, the accuracy of our data, and the strategic importance of our own narrow neck of the research woods (p. 94).

The challenge is thus to express strong convictions without appearing to discourage debate. While making their own argument as compelling as possible, academic writers must also acknowledge that divergent views – what Hyland (2000: 12) calls the "plurality of competing interpretations" – may be equally valid, and are certainly welcome. To achieve the right balance, they mobilise persuasive power, making "a series of rhetorical choices to galvanise support, express collegiality, resolve difficulties and avoid disagreement" (Hyland 2000: 13). The second of these rhetorical purposes (expressing collegiality) reminds us how persuasion requires a writer to enter into a sort of (mock-)conversation with their readers (Booth et al. 2016: 110-111) in which they 'speak' the words of both parties.

Yet even the most persuasive rhetoric will prove unconvincing if readers cannot easily follow the argument it is supposed to serve. This is why good writers help their readers find their way through what, after all, is a complex text. Their assistance is not entirely altruistic, however. They map the route rather like many an experienced tour guide does, taking their group to some of the sites but not all of them. In the same way, a writer directs their readers' attention selectively, highlighting certain parts of their text but downplaying others. Guidance is thus inevitably intertwined with persuasion.

The close relationship between the two has led Hyland (2000, 2017) to apply an umbrella concept that covers both: metadiscourse. It includes some linguistic resources that he terms "organisational" in nature (e.g., references to other parts of the text) and others that are "evaluative", and thus persuasive. Hyland makes a strong case for his very broad definition, while also developing a fine-grained taxonomy of the resources involved. In light of our readers' likely needs, however, we have decided to adopt the approach favoured by Ädel & Mauranen (2010: 2) and restricted the *meta* label to the organisational (i.e., guidance) elements. To avoid confusion with Hyland's terminology, we will refer to these as *metacomments*.

WHAT'S COMING UP

7.1   Showing the reader the way: Metacomments
7.2   Getting the reader on your side
    7.2.1   Reasoning
    7.2.2   Emphasising
    7.2.3   Evaluating
    7.2.4   Rapport-building

7.1 Showing the reader the way: Metacomments

Throughout the book, we have emphasised the need to support the reader, for example by fulfilling their genre expectations, clearing a path through complex sentences, and making it easy to spot the links between ideas. In this section, we focus on another type of device that has a similar supportive role: what we have decided to call *metacomments*. These are remarks, not about the text content, but rather about how the writer is approaching that content. Among other things, they tell readers:

- what a particular passage is meant to do (*the point I am making is ...*);
- which stage in the argument has been reached (*having discussed X ...*);
- where the text is headed next (*we will now move on to Y*).

They are, in effect, signposts for the reader, showing them the way through the text.

As with all linguistic features, individual writers use metacomments to different extents. Some use them sparingly, whereas others (such as the author quoted in Extract 7.2) deploy them liberally. Generally speaking, though, such authorial interventions are widespread in English academic writing and, up to a point, expected; if a text provides no such guidance at all, readers can easily feel adrift. It is thus definitely a practice to be adopted – with the usual proviso that it is not to be overdone. Below are two good examples.

TYPICAL METACOMMENTS

Extract 7.1 [Lewis 2021: 322]
I first survey the literature around the mobilities turn and emphasise its implications for social science research, **before turning to** how policy mobilities theories and methodologies can be employed within policy sociology.

Extract 7.2 [Attfield 2016]
Before more is said, a few words are in place to clarify the notions of progress and of directionality. [...] (p. 30)
Here it would be appropriate to comment that [...]. (p. 38)
To revert now to the topic of progress in science, [...]. (p. 41)
As for progress in organic nature, **that is the topic of the coming section**. [...] (p. 43)
Let us now return to evolution, to consider whether [...]. (p. 43)
Some reflections on this state of affairs **are offered in the section that follows**. [...] (p. 46)
Before we turn to conclusions, **it is worth considering** [...]. (p. 48)

The examples above are fairly simple structuring devices, looking back in the text or, as advance organisers, looking ahead. (Clearly, there is a close connection, even overlap, with some of the cohesive devices discussed in 5.2.4.)

However, as the next set of examples shows, metacomments can also make a more substantive contribution, situating a piece of research or one step in an argument in a broader context and highlighting why it is significant. In such cases, clusters of several authorial interventions are not unusual (see Extracts 7.4 and 7.5), and the organising and evaluative functions are intertwined. (So, Hyland's approach, keeping them both under the same conceptual roof, is vindicated after all – as is our decision to cover them in a single chapter.)

METACOMMENTS COMBINED WITH SCHOLARLY ARGUMENTS

Extract 7.3 [Shipp 2021: 357]
The issue of the war **must again be brought to the forefront here,** particularly on account of Southey.

Extract 7.4 [Jones, H. 2019: 194]
Property and territory are both historically produced practices for ordering space. (...) **To understand** the limits of these practices, **it is necessary to understand** their historic contingency. **The rest of this paper turns to** that history, both in England and its colonies, in the broad context of the transition from feudalism to capitalism.

Extract 7.5 [Fu & Cooper 2021: 439]
In this research, we suggest that *nonprofit network portfolios* offer insights into how managers might structure their partnerships strategically as they pursue organizational and collective goals. To extend our knowledge of how NPOs can configure their ego networks in a strategic manner, **this study centers** around two interlocking research questions (RQs): (1) What network portfolios do different NPOs maintain? (2) What are some influencing factors?

    In the following sections, we first introduce the concept of *nonprofit network portfolios* – the patterns (*number, integration, intensity,* and *duration*) of a set of interorganizational relations that organizations maintain as a whole – based on prior social and interorganizational network research. **This shifts theoretical focus** from the dyadic- and network-level of analysis of partnerships to egocentric analysis of focal organizations. **We then describe** two factors, financial resources and social mission, thought to be related to nonprofit networking. **Next, we describe** the method and the results of the analysis based on surveys from 452 NPOs.

The value of metacomments, whatever their type, is always open to debate. By way of a brief experiment, try removing them from one of the above extracts. The core message will still be there, but it will be more difficult for readers to process. They will have to work out for themselves how the ideas are related and where the argument is going: a burden that in English academic writing they should not have to bear. What is more, they will get less of a sense that the author is 'present' and talking to them personally – an effect that English academic writing sets great store by (see 7.2.4).

Metacomments need not have the grammatical form of declaratives; they may also be formulated as imperatives (instructions). These, though, are largely formulaic and not 'interactive' in the true sense of the word. Still, if you convert any of the following examples to a version without an imperative (e.g., *there are two contrasting examples*), you will see that the solution adopted by the author does indeed engage the reader more.

METACOMMENTS USING IMPERATIVES
Extract 7.6 [Taylor 2020: 179]
Consider two contrasting examples for illustration of the claim that empty categories can be indispensable to inquiry.

Extract 7.7 [Seuren et al. 2021: 64]
Take the following extract from a video consultation between a patient with heart failure and his specialist nurse (...).

Extract 7.8 [Evans 2020: 881]
To understand my claims, **let us return** to the late 1960s and examine the possible entities that could interpret the views of the public.

Finally, readers can also be guided with the help of direct questions indicating that a new stage in the argument is about to begin, as in these examples.

METACOMMENTS USING DIRECT QUESTIONS
Extract 7.9 [Collier & Cox 2021: 290]
What are the implications of our analysis for broader discussions of the politics of resilience?

Extract 7.10 [Jones, S. 2018: 147]
Why did English dramatists look to French plays for translation sources from the 1660s onwards? The answer lies in part in the turbulent political background of the mid seventeenth century.

Extract 7.11 [Loges 2021: 14]

How might such a concert have been experienced by an audience? **Would they have heard** its contents as related or entirely separate? Answering this question forces us into what might be described as "subjunctive theory."[63]

Such questions are merely rhetorical, of course, but they create a semblance of interactivity that comes across as lively and reader-centred. Thus, as well as helping to structure the text, direct questions create rapport (see 7.2.4).

7.2 Getting the reader on your side

In this section, we will be looking at a range of strategies employed by writers to persuade readers that their various claims (i.e., assertions) are valid ones. This being a vast subject, we will pick out four strategies used by writers to get readers on their side. The first is reasoning, a concept we will define and discuss in the first subsection below. Next we will examine emphasising: the various means by which authors lay stress on particular parts of a text. Third comes evaluation, which involves assessing relevant theories and methods as well as other people's research, while additionally bringing to bear the writer's own perspective on the social and cultural phenomena in question. And finally we will consider the personal dimension, the writer's attempts to win over his or her readers by establishing a positive rapport with them. Of course, our compartmentalisation of strategies is purely an analytical tool. In reality, and in the hands of a skilled writer, all four work in harness, reinforcing each other to achieve the best persuasive results.

7.2.1 Reasoning

By *reasoning* we mean constructing an argument in favour of a specific claim while deflating potential objections to it. In English, this process is a form of ritualised game played by a writer and their readers. The former 'pretends' not to know whether the claim is justified and to be 'thinking it through' for her- or himself. Meanwhile, the readers play along and 'accept' the reasoning as their own.

The chain of causality

The first element of reasoning, as we use the term here, is a chain of causes (or reasons) and effects (or outcomes) supporting the writer's claim. Extract 7.12 provides a good example.

A CAUSAL CHAIN OF REASONING

Extract 7.12 [Neff 2022: 3]

The U.K. appears to occupy a position somewhere between Hallin and Mancini's Liberal and Democratic Corporatist models because its media system features a broadcast sector that includes the BBC, which, as the world's largest public media outlet, is an icon of state intervention in media markets.

Here, the author's claim is made in the initial part of the sentence (*The U.K. appears ... models*). The immediate reason is the fact that Britain's *broadcast sector includes the BBC*. And that, in turn, is backed up by the fact that the BBC is *an icon of state intervention in media markets.*

In this case, the causal chain is a simple one with only two components, but in others it may be much longer. The following extract is a case in point; the chain it describes is actually a four-part one. We are told: that competitive advantage in Information and Communications Technology (ICT) has led to the creation of superstar companies; that this development has increased market concentration and the accumulation of digital capital in a few hands; that this accumulation has led to a degree of monopoly; and that monopoly power leads to inequality. And all that, as is perfectly natural, within a single paragraph.

A LONGER CAUSAL CHAIN

Extract 7.13 [Spence 2021: 4]

Competitive advantage in ICT and intangible capital, including data, **has given birth to** superstar companies (Autor et al., 2020). These companies are characterized by high added value and low labor share, **resulting in** a significant increase in market concentration and a decline in labor income. Most "superstar companies" have accumulated a great deal of digital capital – factors of production that are complementary to recorded investments in IT assets (such as hardware and software), but that are not otherwise recorded on a firm's balance sheets

– which **leads to** a certain degree of monopoly (Tambe et al., 2020). This monopoly power **may** then **create** or aggravate the inequality of access to private data and lead to further predatory or discriminatory pricing behavior.

You will also have noted that this chain runs in the opposite direction, as it were. In other words, it does not *begin* with a claim but *builds up to* one – which, in terms of end focus at least (see 3.2.2), is often a more effective strategy.

Such long chains are not difficult to understand, as such; but it is absolutely vital that the fundamental principle of linearity is observed (see 2.2.2). If it is not – and, say, 'A leads to C, and C leads to B' – then readers lose their bearings. Makeover 7.1 shows an (invented) example of this unwanted effect, as well as a means of avoiding it. In the *Before* sentence, the immediate cause of the company's falling sales is given as *the economic problems in key overseas markets*. However, that is actually the underlying reason. A key link has been omitted: the reason why these unspecified 'economic problems' should have affected the retailer's sales (i.e., the immediate cause). That link is supplied in the sentence's final clause, breaking the chain's linearity; the reader is brought back from their journey's destination to a point along the way. In the *After* version, this problem is resolved by reversing the order of the underlying and immediate reasons, thus restoring linearity.

MAKEOVER 7.1: ORDERING A CHAIN OF REASONING CORRECTLY

Before
The retailer has experienced a sales slump because of the economic problems in key overseas markets, which have massively cut disposable incomes there.

After
The retailer has experienced a sales slump because of massive cuts to disposable incomes in key overseas markets. These cuts have, in turn, resulted from the economic problems there.

Whatever shape or form such a chain may take, it is bound to depend heavily on the language of causality to link its various parts. In Extract 7.12, the claim is connected to the immediate reason by *because*, while the underlying reason is contained in a relative clause. In Extract 7.13, where the causal chain runs in the opposite direction (i.e., it leads up to the claim), the chain is held together by four verbal expressions signalling outcomes (*has given birth to; resulting in; leads to* and *may create*). Naturally, these are not the only ways to join up causal chains. Toolbox 7.1 provides a selection of the most common linguistic devices used to do that.

Toolbox 7.1 **CONSTRUCTING CAUSAL CHAINS**	
1. Reasons/causes	
Linkers	*as; because; for; since*
Verbs	*be brought about by; be caused by; derive from; reflect;* *result from*
Nouns	*cause; reason; root*
2. Outcomes/effects	
Linkers	*accordingly; as a result; consequently; hence; so; therefore; thus*
Verbs	*bring about; entail; generate; give rise to; lead to; mean*
Nouns	*consequence; effect; impact; outcome; repercussion; result*

Concessions and the 'Yes, but' strategy

As you will probably have noticed, there has not been much evidence yet of the 'conversation' we mentioned at the start of the chapter. What we have described so far is essentially a monologue, not something likely to prove very persuasive to an informed and critical audience. As Booth et al. (2016: 141) put it, "if you give your readers only claims, reasons, and evidence – no matter how compelling these are to you – they may still find your argument thin or, worse, ignorant or dismissive of their views". Instead, participants in the academic debate must be prepared to proactively engage with other points of view and indeed criticisms. In other words, writers must let their readers have a say – if only through the writer's own words.

Academic texts must therefore provide pegs on which criticism and debate can be hung. "As paradoxical as it seems, you make your argument stronger and more credible by modestly acknowledging its limits" (Booth et al. 2016: 129). In order to do that, you must be willing to 'write as a reader' as the common saying goes, anticipating readers' potential objections to your arguments, conceding their validity and only then refuting them.

Provided an objection is short, this can be done within a single sentence beginning with one of the standard concessive linkers (*although, (even) though* or *even if*). However, if the objection is longer, or if there are several potential objections relating to the same point, this will no longer be grammatically possible – and, in any case, it would place too great a burden on the reader. So what is to be done? This is where the 'Yes, but' strategy comes in, and the following two extracts show it being used in its standard form.

THE 'YES, BUT' STRATEGY: STANDARD FORMAT

Extract 7.14 [Scales 2022: 325]
It is true that the same formative high medieval tensions, between cosmopolitanism and particularism, expanding horizons and local worlds, could also be fruitfully explored by focusing on other spheres of life, such as popular religious practice or changing economic relations. Cultural unities (and their antitheses) do, **however**, command a special importance, simply because some of the most influential modern judgments on the period have identified unity as its defining characteristic and claim to significance.

Extract 7.15 [Parker & Thomas 2011: 421][1]
Of course many academics would argue that all good work in the social sciences is critical, in the sense of being sceptical of common sense, and regarding all arguments as provisional and dependent on evidence. This is fair enough, **but** here we are specifically interested in disciplinary developments in the English speaking academic world which self-consciously claim dissent as their distinctiveness.

As is evident from these extracts, the structure is the same as for a simple concession: first objection, then refutation. What is different is the way in which the two are connected. Between objection and refutation, the authors have placed what one might call an *argumentative linker*: *however* in the first extract and *but* in the second. Such linkers indicate not only a contrast of

---

1   In this extract, many writers would have put a comma after *of course* and spelt *English speaking* with a hyphen.

some sort; they also tell the reader to consider what comes after them to be weightier than what came before. That is the 'but' part of the strategy.

The 'Yes' part was an earlier concessive linker (*it is true that* in Extract 7.14 and *of course* in Extract 7.15), which alerted the reader to look out for the upcoming argumentative one. Linkers like *it is true* or *admittedly* differ from *although* and co because their effect 'reaches' into the next sentence – and beyond. As a result, these 'long-reach' linkers can be used to create concessive structures that extend over several sentences, and even across paragraph boundaries. In Toolbox 7.2, you will find some of the most common examples of the various linker types used to make and refute concessions in academic writing.

Toolbox 7.2 **LINKERS USED IN CONCESSIVE STRUCTURES**	
Concessive	*although; even though; even if; though*
Concessive ('long-reach')	*admittedly; certainly; for sure; it is true (that); of course*
Argumentative	*but; however; nevertheless; nonetheless; still; though;*[2] *yet*
Contrastive	*by contrast; in contrast; on the other hand*

Our next two examples illustrate how the standard 'Yes, but' pattern can be varied creatively.

VARIATIONS ON THE 'YES, BUT' FORMAT

Extract 7.16 [Lipson 2013: 271]
Edward Schiappa suggested in 2003 that in historical rhetorical study, an individual scholar will "find most salient" those elements that connect with his/her own interests (210). **That is true. Yet** scholars also function in specific cultural contexts.

Extract 7.17 [Mackin 2022: 782]
I do not deny that this consensus captures important parts of Habermas's account. Habermas does associate communicative power with

---

2   *Though* must be handled with great care. If placed in the middle of a clause, its force is argumentative. If it comes at the clause's beginning, it is concessive, just like *although* (e.g., *though these results are impressive, they remain tentative*).

the formation of a common will, and he uses the concept to explain how popular sovereignty is possible. **Still,** it is not quite right to argue that Habermas presents communicative power only as a will that happens to be formed communicatively.

In Extract 7.16, the concessive linker (*that is true*) comes not at the start of the objection but in a short punchy sentence following it. And the author of Extract 7.17 has indicated the concession, not by a linker, but by the phrase *I do not deny that,* which serves the same concessive function while also helping to establish rapport with the readership (see 7.2.4).

The examples of the 'Yes, but' strategy we have examined so far have all been extremely forceful ones. Sometimes, however, an author may wish to back up a more tentative claim, as in this example. (Note how it ends: ... *is not entirely appropriate.*)

'YES, BUT' STRATEGY IN SUPPORT OF A TENTATIVE CLAIM
Extract 7.18 [Attfield 2016: 36]
Admittedly the kinds of directionality here do not involve progress towards goals agreed antecedently. **On the other hand** we can recognise directionality towards implicit goals such as survival, enhanced ways of coping with a given environment, and adaptability to a wider range of environments. Development towards these implicit goals is readily recognisable among species and organisms. So **talk about progressive development in nature is not entirely inappropriate**.

Presumably, that is why the author has not used a middle linker of the argumentative type (such as *however*), but a contrastive one *(on the other hand)* which says nothing about the relative weights of the preceding objection and the subsequent refutation. Nonetheless, the paragraph structure (first objection, then refutation) makes clear which side of the argument he stands on (and that, for rhetorical reasons, had to come last).

To wrap up our discussion of reasoning, we should recall that we have been talking throughout about sustaining a claim and how this involves talking one side up and another one down. However, if the point of a passage is to present both sides of an argument as being essentially in balance, then it is best to avoid both concessive and argumentative linkers – precisely because they indicate a preference for one side or the other. Instead, more neutral linkers such as *by/in contrast* or *on the other hand* are needed. And for this more balanced perspective, a 'point-counterpoint' approach is exactly what is required.

In Brief
COMMON PATTERNS OF REASONING IN ENGLISH TEXTS

- Causal chains connecting claims and the grounds for them
- Concessions to potential objections
- An objection-refutation structure involving a concessive linker
- The 'Yes, but' strategy, which also involves an argumentative linker (e.g., *however*)

7.2.2 Emphasising

In the previous section, we discussed how, in constructing a reasoned argument, writers may emphasise some points rather than others. However, that is by no means the only context in which they will wish to make use of emphasis. They can do so in a variety of ways. At the higher levels of textual organisation, an issue can be stressed by giving it the status of a headed (sub)section, or at least its own paragraph; at the word level, adjectives such as *important* or *crucial* can be used (more on both of these points in 7.2.3). But the key level in this regard is probably that of the sentence. In Section 3.2.2, we discussed how, in general, a piece of information placed at the sentence end is assigned greater importance than one that comes earlier. Here, we will look at two specific structures that similarly lend emphasis to a particular point.

Inversion

Inversion is an exception to the strict rules governing word order in English. It is accordingly to be used with immense care. However, under certain, highly restricted circumstances, inversion is possible – and very useful. Here are three typical examples.

INVERSION IN ACTION
Extract 7.19 [Turner & Blackie 2018: 200]
The Industrial Revolution produced injury, illness and disablement on a large scale and **nowhere was this more visible** than in coalmining.

Extract 7.20 [Haire & MacDonald 2019: 278]
Authors Gooding (2016) and Stewart (2000) underlined the importance
of a sense of humour for music therapists in their professional lives.
Not only was it observed as one of many essential "career-sustaining
strategies" (Gooding, 2016, p. 5), it was also noted as a positive personal
characteristic when seeking to collaborate with other professionals or
create new music therapy work (Stewart, 2000).

Extract 7.21 [Leduc, Kubler & Georges 2021: 1]
This paper highlights the fact that most of today's blockchain-based
farming frameworks focus on food tracking and traceability. **Only
rarely does** research focus on the design of digital marketplaces
to support the trading of agricultural goods between farmers and
potentially interested third party stakeholders; **equally rarely are**
performance evaluations performed for the proposed frameworks.

As these three extracts show, inversion involves moving to the start of a
sentence an element that is either negative (e.g., *not only,*[3] *never* or *nowhere*)
or "restrictive" (e.g., *hardly* or *rarely*; Biber et al. 1999: 915). The result is to
invert (i.e., reverse) the usual positions of subject and verb.[4] The effect is
one of very strong emphasis, especially because inversion is so unusual and
thus really stands out. The flip side, as always, is that the technique can only
be used sparingly since otherwise the intended effect wears off. Or, worse
still, repeated use of the pattern may grate on the reader, so that they are
antagonised instead of won over.

The second scenario occurs when an adjective or adjectival phrase is put
at the very beginning of a sentence, a technique known as "fronting" (Biber
et al. 1999: 902-905). Illustrated in Extracts 7.22 and 7.23, it is even rarer than
the first, and once again, perhaps for that very reason, it has great rhetorical
power.

---

3   *Not only* is a complex case because inversion may or may not occur depending on the
     contrast that is being drawn. Compare these two sentences: *Not only is this argument
     illogical, it is (also) based on false premises* versus *Not only this argument is illogical; so
     too are all the others in which it is embedded.*
4   More precisely, the subject and the auxiliary verb (*will, would, has, did,* etc.) are reversed.
     If the verb phrase does not include an auxiliary, the appropriate form of *do* has to be
     supplied, as is done in the first inversion included in Extract 7.21.

FRONTING
Extract 7.22 [Scales 2022: 350]
Fundamentally important to the development of high medieval European identities **was** the 'investiture contest' of the late eleventh and early twelfth centuries.[171]

Extract 7.23 [Das 2019: 342]
Similarly, the prose writers of the fifth and fourth century show an equal, and in some cases more invested, interest in medical language. **Notable are** Thucydides and Plato.[7]

According to Biber et al. (1999: 902), fronting "contain[s] an element of comparison with respect to the preceding context". Thus, the arrangement is also in keeping with the given-new principle.

Cleft sentences
Another important way of emphasising a particular element is by means of cleft sentences. These are so-called because a single clause is cleft (i.e., split) into two separate clauses. The desired emphasis is achieved by delaying the sentence element which the author wishes to stress.

There are two main types of cleft sentences. The first are referred to as *it-clefts* for reasons that will be obvious from these two extracts.

CLEFT SENTENCES (#1)
Extract 7.24 [Delanty 2022: 4]
It was Foucault who replaced Adorno as the really major thinker of the 1970s.

Extract 7.25 [Scales 2022: 350]
It was precisely the most 'universal', pan-European cultural currents of the central Middle Ages that did most to give voice, and a more explicit form, to the identities, claims and titles of many communities.

In Extract 7.24, where the corresponding simple sentence would run *Foucault replaced Adorno as ...*, *Foucault* becomes *It was Foucault*. In Extract 7.25, the lengthy subject (*the most 'universal' ... Middle Ages*) is similarly delayed, making the sentence decidedly more emphatic.

The other main cleft type is known as a *wh-cleft* because it makes use of one of the *wh*-words (the question words beginning with *wh*, along with *how*). The next three extracts provide examples.

CLEFT SENTENCES (#2)

Extract 7.26 [Das 2019: 346-347]
Ultimately, **what** made Hippocratic medicine attractive was its optimism.

Extract 7.27 [Harrison, Hole & Habibi 2020: 672]
Previous research has demonstrated several own-group biases (OGBs) in face recognition, but **why** they occur is unclear.

Extract 7.28 [Adger & Trousdale 2007: 263]
Note that this perspective allows us to study language independently of the minds that produce the linguistic system: **all we need** is a theory of the system itself.

In Extract 7.26, for example, *optimism made Hippocratic medicine attractive* becomes *what made Hippocratic medicine attractive was its optimism*, while in Extract 7.27 *why they occur* effectively replaces *the reason*. The third example shows that clefts starting with *all* follow the same pattern as the *wh*-variety.

In some cases, a cleft can be combined with other means of emphasis, as in the next example, where it contributes to the second part of a 'Yes, but' structure (see 7.2.1). Also noteworthy is the emphasis lent to the first part, the 'objection', by the use of *we do expect*.

CLEFT COMBINED WITH ANOTHER MEANS OF EMPHASIS

Extract 7.29 [Munno et al. 2022: 67]
We do expect the more engaged, empathetic mindset that emerged in this study to persist in a larger population. **What we cannot know, however,** is what additional mindsets might emerge, especially as we pivot toward conducting this study with professional journalists as the participants, which is the next step in this research.

The emphatic nature of cleft sentences comes particularly into its own when they are placed in salient positions within a paragraph. The clefts in Extracts 7.26 and 7.27, for instance, are both topic sentences that begin their respective paragraphs. Another typical location is at the beginning of a concluding sentence, as in this example.

CLEFT ADDING EMPHASIS TO A PARAGRAPH'S FINAL SENTENCE
Extract 7.30 [Hyde 2020: 228]
While there is some evidence to suggest that (for the self-styled godly at least) these cultures had diverged by the seventeenth century, the mid-sixteenth century witnessed the zenith of the godly ballad.[58] Though they contained only a limited amount of theologically accurate teaching, they found an audience among those who wanted to fuse recreation with an appearance of piety.[59] **What they did not do, however**, was include musical notation on the printed sheets.

7.2.3 Evaluating

As well as being an important argumentative tool in its own right, emphasising also contributes to the third dimension of academic persuasion: evaluating. This brings in the writer's own perspective, and thus inevitably a subjective element – which, however, must not be confused with outright bias. In general usage, evaluation is associated mainly with the word level, and in particular with adjectives that describe things as good, bad, or something in between: *amazing, horrific* or *nice*, for instance. In academic argumentation, you will not be surprised to hear, things aren't quite so simple.

For a start, evaluation takes place not only along a 'good versus bad' scale, but also on other, equally relevant scales such as 'certain versus uncertain' or 'important versus unimportant' (where emphasising comes in). Think of a discussion section trying to make sense of empirical findings. In their concluding assessment, the author will want to distinguish more important results from less important ones; they will be more confident about some results than others; and yes, they may reflect on the social impact of their research and in that respect, too, make value judgements.

What is more, evaluation is not necessarily easy to identify. It can be subtle and indirect, hinted at rather than stated explicitly. Nor is it always a question of black and white; instead, academic argument is more likely to unfold in the grey area in between. Unless a momentous paradigm shift is imminent, the competition of ideas is generally quite muted, progress is incremental, and persuasion generally an understated affair. Accordingly, evaluative resources in academic writing are often low key – and all the more difficult to master as a result.

With academic evaluation being so multi-faceted, and the space available in our chapter limited, we have decided to focus on linguistic features that our teaching experience suggests will be particularly relevant for our audience. We will begin at the word level and work up to the sentence, paragraph and text levels.

Word choice

Words do not 'mean' only what the dictionary says. They also carry an evaluative load: a semantic baggage of sometimes fuzzy associations putting a spin on the person or thing described. It may be tempting to think that academic writing is somehow above the fuzziness, and that may indeed be true as far as technical terminology is concerned (though such terms, too, may be heavily contested and anything but unambiguous). But where academic writing uses non-technical language, authors are up against the same questions as everyone else. If there are synonyms to choose from, which one best expresses my 'take' on things? Which words are most likely to persuade my readers that they should adopt my point of view? And how can I use word choice to distinguish between things I approve or disapprove of, and between views that I am more certain or less certain about?

There have been glimpses of the challenges involved at various points in our book, and specifically in Chapter 6, where we talked about the connotations of different reporting verbs. Here, we would like to focus on certain types of lexical resources which play a key role in signalling to the reader where the author stands. We will begin with so-called hedges and boosters, which as Hyland puts it (2000: 87), enable a writer "to invest a convincing degree of assurance in their propositions", and yet "to avoid overstating their case and risk inviting the rejection of their arguments".

Hedges are words and phrases that express the writer's lack of certainty about a particular statement and/or weaken the statement itself in some way. After all, however competently a piece of research has been carried out, it may not be possible to report completely watertight findings. Data may be messy, evidence contradictory and interpretations speculative. In all these cases, and especially when it comes to discussing results or drawing final conclusions, researchers often prefer to make their statements sound tentative to some extent.

Hedging devices may take a variety of linguistic forms. These include both modal verbs (in particular those expressing varying degrees of uncertainty, namely *may* and *might*, *should* and *ought to*) and ordinary verbs with meanings close to modals (e.g., *seem*, *appear*, *suggest*). Alternatively, hedges may be adjectives such as *potential*, adverbs such as *perhaps*, or nouns such as *possibility*. As the following extracts from the discussion sections of papers show, several such devices can be combined.

HEDGES
Extract 7.31 [Winchenbach, Hanna & Miller 2022: 9]
Seeing diversification this way **might help** address concerns over identity and dignity threats in diversification (Brookfield et al., 2005).

Extract 7.32 [Shimpo, Wesener & McWilliam 2019: 130]
Any attempt to generalise our data beyond the case is **speculative** and additional (comparative) studies are needed to substantiate findings. However, based on those **preliminary** findings, the paper **suggests** that both pre- and (temporary) post-disaster community gardens **may play** important roles in the immediate disaster recovery period following the earthquakes.

Boosters, on the other hand, have the opposite effect. They show that the writer is strongly committed to a statement, or wishes to strengthen the statement itself in some way. Again, modal verbs play a key role, though from the other end of the spectrum, expressing certainty (*must* and *will*). Adverbs also contribute (e.g., *clearly*, *undoubtedly*) as do related phrases that include nouns (e.g., *there can be no doubt that ...*).

BOOSTERS
Extract 7.33 [du Plessis 2021: 3]
It is **undoubtedly** true that the law degree is a professional qualification designed to equip students for a career in the various branches of the legal profession.

Extract 7.34 [Miller 2022: 315]
It is **essential** to draw this distinction between natural and artificial duties of rescue because the shape that they take may be quite different, including over the significance of the rescuee's responsibility.

Extract 7.35 [Mahn et al. 2022: n. pag.]
This is supported by a **vast** body of evidence on the positive effect of education on performance and thus growth (Van Der Sluis et al., 2008).

Toolbox 7.3 SELECTED HEDGES AND BOOSTERS		
Modals	Hedges	*may; might; could; should; ought to*
	Boosters	*will; must*
Adjectives	Hedges	*possible; probable; slight; moderate*
	Boosters	*considerable; substantial; vast; essential*
Adverbs	Hedges	*seemingly; somewhat; perhaps*
	Boosters	*certainly; inevitably; highly; dramatically*
Adverbials	Hedges	*to a degree; to some extent; up to a point*
	Boosters	*beyond any doubt; with absolute certainty*

Finally in this category come attitude markers. They do 'what it says on the tin', making the author's attitude explicit. They may take the form of full sentences such as *this result is surprising*, but frequently they are condensed into so-called stance adverbials such as *surprisingly*. Below are a few authentic examples.

ATTITUDE MARKERS
Extract 7.36 [Monteiro & Adler 2022: 452]
Sadly, bureaucracy continues to be understood in essentialized terms.

Extract 7.37 [Harris & Leeming 2022: 5]
Finally, **and rather worryingly**, the legitimacy of some of the studies is questionable.

Extract 7.38 [Shipp 2021: 352]
Britishness, **evidently**, was not something simple, single or coherent.

Extract 7.39 [Pösö 2022: 53]
Hardly surprisingly, consent is seen as controversial in many practice settings.

The last two show how some of these stance adverbials have an almost dialogic touch. Although *evidently* and *hardly surprisingly* are about the writer's attitude, they are equally about an imagined conversation with the reader, appealing to shared knowledge – like a brief aside saying 'I know that you know'.

The sentence and paragraph levels - and beyond

All of the above discussion must be tempered by an important reservation; it is not individual words that have evaluative loads, but how they are used in specific contexts: for instance, preceded by a qualifying adverb or negation such as *barely, not entirely,* etc. And of course, words are only ever part of a whole range of evaluative resources. The latter can be located at all linguistic levels, the next being the sentence.

In Section 7.2.2, we saw how certain sentence structures can be used to emphasise particular points, thereby contributing to evaluation. But these are far from the only ones. In fact, all the structural properties of sentences that we discussed in Chapter 3 can be seen to have some persuasive potential.

In the following list, we therefore recap on the main points we made there, stressing now their evaluative contribution rather than their structural features.

- Short, simple sentences can drive points home forcefully; their rhetorical effect is particularly noticeable when they are preceded and followed by longer sentences.
- Following the principle of end focus, one can highlight a piece of information merely by placing it at the end of a clause.
- Opting for a passive construction is often the best means of achieving end focus – and is thus an important tool for displaying information in a way that best suits the writer's persuasive intentions.
- Using plenty of verbs, and keeping abstract nouns to the necessary minimum, livens sentences up – and so increases their impact.

And, overall, if you lose your readers' attention, you have effectively thrown away the opportunity to persuade them.

At the paragraph level, too, structure has an important evaluative task to perform. For example, varying sentence structures and sentence beginnings within a paragraph improves the flow (see 2.3). Consequently, rather than having to plod on unaided, readers are carried along by the argument – in itself a contribution to persuasive effect.

But there is more to it than that. First, given what we said in Chapter 2 about the structure of English paragraphs, it stands to reason that a key role in evaluation falls to the topic sentence. Typically, this says not only what the paragraph will discuss, but also from what angle it will do so. In the following example, the topic sentence raises an argument about the *fragility of social categories* (*one might expect* ...), but the *might* tells us immediately that the paragraph will be about refuting it (see 7.2.1).

TOPIC SENTENCE INDICATING AN ATTITUDE TO UPCOMING CONTENT
Extract 7.40 [Taylor 2020: 173-174]
One might expect the fragility of social categories to be correlated with their explanatory indispensability, such that the more fragile a social category is, the less likely it is to be explanatorily indispensable. **But** this is not the case, as remarkably fragile categories can be indispensable to explanations of certain social phenomena. (...)

In that case, the evaluative signal in the topic sentence was pretty hard to miss. In others, such signals can be more muted, and yet unmistakably persuasive.

A SUBTLY EVALUATIVE TOPIC SENTENCE
Extract 7.41 [Loges 2021: 6]
Over the last half century, much scholarship has sought to explain and thereby affirm the cyclical coherence of *Winterreise*, often requiring the assembling of formidable theoretical arsenals.[25]

Here, the disagreement with previous scholarship is only hinted at in an ironical manner. After all, an argument can't be all that convincing if it requires *formidable theoretical arsenals* to back it up. Note how the metaphor (*arsenal*) further enhances the irony. Word choice also contributes to the subtle disparagement; other scholars merely *sought to explain and thereby affirm*, which is clearly much weaker than *explained and affirmed* would have been, implying that ultimately these other scholars weren't successful. The result is a powerful topic sentence which sets the tone for the paragraph, suggests an authoritative voice and draws the reader in with vivid imagery.

At the paragraph level, too, writers make evaluative decisions, the first being whether to give a particular idea the honour of its own separate paragraph. Conversely, a writer may choose to downplay an issue by denying it a separate paragraph, instead dealing with it in one or two sentences somewhere in the middle of a paragraph devoted to a broader idea. Writers make such evaluative moves all the time, just as they constantly experiment with different paragraph structures – upgrading and downgrading the relevance of arguments, and moving sentences around within them – in order to maximise the whole text's impact and getting the reader to see the world their way.

Going still further up the hierarchy, you can assign a theme particular importance by giving it its own headed subsection or section (or, in the case of a book, its own chapter). Alternatively, you might decide during the revision process that an issue previously singled out in this way does not in fact deserve such high status, in which case you will wish to downgrade it by a level or two: from a section to a subsection, or from there to a paragraph (or even just a couple of sentences).

7.2.4 Rapport-building

Last but far from least, we turn to the question of how writers can make their readers more susceptible to persuasion by establishing rapport with them. We have already touched on one method, during the discussion of stance adverbials in the previous section. There it was *evidently* and *hardly surprisingly* that were identified as indicative of an appeal to knowledge shared by writer and readers; other adverbs with similar effects are *clearly, obviously* and *naturally*. Their related adjectives are also used, as in this example.

> **APPEAL TO SHARED KNOWLEDGE**
> **Extract 7.42** [Jones, H. 2019: 193]
> Property relies on the state for recognition and formalisation, **that much is obvious.**

Alternatively, an inclusive *we*, used to refer jointly to the author(s) and the reader, can be used to achieve the same effect (e.g., *as we can see from this table; let us now turn to a related point*). Even a sole author can use *we* in this way; what she or he is not supposed to do these days is to use *we* to refer only to themselves, as was once common practice. That really is restricted to authorial teams now. Addressing the reader directly as *you* is also possible, but it is often considered problematic in academic writing and tends to be avoided.

That brings us to one of the most frequently asked questions in academic writing courses: *Is it ok to use* I *in a research paper?* The best answer at this stage, more appropriate than either *no way* or *anything goes* is actually *maybe*, infuriatingly non-committal as that is. Here we will try to add a touch of decisiveness.

You may recall that some of the metacomments cited in Section 7.1 used the first-person pronoun *I* (e.g., *First, I survey ...*), whereas others seemed to studiously avoid it, resorting instead to impersonal expressions (e.g., *it is worth considering...*). Practices clearly vary, which is why it is difficult to give general advice. What we can say, though, is that *I* is no longer completely taboo. (By analogy, the same applies to *my, mine* and *me*.) Some academics still cannot bring themselves to use it, true, and also advise their students against it. But increasingly a more relaxed attitude appears to be gaining ground.

Nonetheless, two warnings are in order. First, *I* is still quite a 'marked' stylistic choice. In other words, it stands out, and readers notice it more than they would impersonal alternatives. As a result, many writers try to avoid making it even more marked by putting it up front in the sentence, paragraph or section. Instead, they prefer to insert another sentence element before it. All it takes, for example, is a short adverbial in front of *I* to make it less obtrusive. Thus, at the beginning of a paragraph, *In what follows, I compare these two methods* sounds more acceptable than just *I compare these two methods*. The extract below gives an authentic example.

Unobtrusive use of *I*

Extract 7.43 [Ballinger 2022: 7]
This is quite different from, **I would add**, 'the close-ups of legs (Dietrich, for instance) or a face (Garbo)' that creates another level of 'eroticism' in Hollywood films that Mulvey notes (Mulvey 2009, p. 20).

Second, writers tend to avoid several instances of *I* in quick succession. In Methods sections, which describe procedures carried out by the author, such repetition could easily sound very clumsy. In these cases, most authors prefer allowing the passive voice to come to the rescue (see 3.3).

Finally, if you want to avoid *I*, what techniques are available to you? The passive we have already mentioned. A second option is to replace the personal pronoun with an impersonal noun, such as *(this) book, contribution, paper, study, research, work,* or whatever else fits best in the context concerned. So, in an abstract for example, *I suggest* might become *this paper suggests*. A further option is to use an impersonal construction such as *it is argued*, as is done in the following extract.

AVOIDING *I* THROUGH IMPERSONAL CONSTRUCTIONS
Extract 7.44 [Hart 2019: 582]
This paper offers a critical examination of the nature of inequalities in relation to education and the pursuit of social justice. **It argues** that assessment of educational resources and measures such as school enrolment and educational achievement are limited in what they tell us about the injustices learners may experience. **It is proposed that**, drawing on Amartya Sen's capability approach, we benefit from extending our evaluative space beyond learners' achievements to encompass their freedoms to achieve. **It is argued** that attention should be paid to the relative value individuals place on these various freedoms. Furthermore, in order to deepen insights into the multiple factors influencing the development of learner values, and the unequal possibilities for realising their aspired valued achievements, **the discussion also draws on** key sociological concepts from Pierre Bourdieu. **The theoretical synthesis leads to** the introduction of the Sen-Bourdieu Analytical Framework, a conceptual model that illustrates the socially dynamic processes within which learners and formal educational systems are situated. **The principal aims are to** offer an alternative development paradigm and an expanded evaluative framework to inform local, national and international educational policy and practice.

As Extract 7.45 shows, writers may also mix personal and impersonal formulations. Yet again, variety is the name of the game.

MIXING *I* AND IMPERSONAL FORMULATIONS IN AN ABSTRACT
Extract 7.45 [Parker 2018: 178]
This article is concerned with the representation of one particular form of work within popular culture during a particular period, in order to understand just how much representations of work have altered over the past half century. **I discuss** the James Bond phenomenon and the ways in which it has been understood by cultural theorists. **I then**

look at what the novels suggest about understandings of work and organizations in Britain in the 1950s before comparing that period to later Bonds. **The latter operation necessarily involves thinking through** the ways in which an understanding of historical context is crucial to thinking through the production and consumption of any text, whether about work and organizations, or any other topic. **The article concludes with** some thoughts on the impossibility of the Bond novels being written now, when the organization and its executives are assumed to be agents in generalized conspiracies.

Chapter 7: The takeaways

- Both reader guidance and persuasive strategies are central to research writing.
- Guidance, provided through the writer's metacomments, is intended to help readers find their way through the text, but also to draw their attention to some points rather than others.
- Persuasion has at least four different dimensions: reasoning, emphasising, evaluating and building reader rapport.
- Reasoning, which is concerned with sustaining the claims you make and refuting potential objections to them, has two key components:
  - □ causal chains
  - □ concessive structures, in particular the 'Yes, but' strategy
- Emphasis can be achieved either by word choice or through the use of grammatical structures, in particular:
  - □ inversion
  - □ cleft sentences
- Evaluation can also make use of structural devices at the sentence and paragraph levels. However, it relies heavily on words, specifically:
  - □ hedges
  - □ boosters
  - □ attitude markers
- Rapport can be built in various ways, in particular by:
  - □ appealing to shared knowledge or experience
  - □ inserting the author(s) directly into the text through the use of *I* and *we*

Appendix 1
Conference presentations

Although this book is about written academic English, we feel that to say nothing at all about the spoken variety would be distinctly remiss. In this Appendix, we therefore intend to make a few remarks about the latter. Spoken academic English is to be heard in a wide range of contexts: in various traditional forms of semi- or non-structured academic discussion and, increasingly, in virtual meetings. Here, though, we will restrict ourselves to what is perhaps the classic spoken academic genre: a presentation made to a parallel session of a medium- to large-sized international conference.

Clearly such a conference presentation (CP) is very closely related to the type of journal article that has formed the focus of the foregoing chapters. Indeed, the CP will almost certainly be based on such an article, whether already published or in preparation. However, it cannot be merely a 'spoken version' of the article. For one thing, there certainly won't be time for that; typically, you will have 20 minutes to give the CP, and that may include time for discussion. For another, the talk is embedded in the conference as a whole: in the entire array of presentations given there, and in the range of social events that occur during its course.

These contextual issues must be considered in planning and delivering any CP, as of course must the general differences between spoken and written communication. Probably the best place to begin is by looking at two key communication parameters, audience and purpose, which we will now do. Later we will examine some specifically linguistic aspects and also the question of supporting slides (without attempting to give any general tips on presentation technique, an area adequately, if not excessively, covered by a multitude of websites and self-help books).

A1.1 The audience, or 'pity the listener'

Of course, just like the readers of an article, the audience of a CP may vary widely in composition and background. However, that is not our concern here. Instead, we are concerned with the position of listeners in general as opposed to readers, and specifically with listeners to a CP, who are often discouraged from directly interacting with the speaker during the talk. Relative to the readers of a journal article, they thus face several significant disadvantages, which are summed up in the following table.

Readers of an article may ...	Listeners to a CP ...
Re-read more complex passages as they wish.	Have no chance to 're-listen'.
Jump about in the text to remind themselves of its structure.	Must rely on the speaker for structural guidance.
Read at their own pace, pausing whenever they please.	Can take a break only when the speaker does so.

Table A1.1. The relative disadvantages faced by a CP audience

Happily, there are some fairly obvious ways in which you, as a presenter, can come to your audience's aid. Specifically, you can:

■ Introduce redundancy (i.e., material that might be superfluous in writing but is of great help to listeners) by repeating, explaining or paraphrasing difficult terms and passages (see 6.2.1);
■ Provide a 'road-map' at the start and plenty of signposts (the sort of thing discussed in 7.1) along the way;
■ Speak at a relatively slow pace, pausing frequently at appropriate points.

Two comments are in order regarding the last point. First, most people probably speak rather faster than they think, especially when the adrenalin gets going, so when presenting they need to speak at a consciously slow pace. Second, what is an 'appropriate point'? Here, the considerations are much the same as those that apply to punctuating written texts; pauses should never come in the middle of an idea but always at a natural break in the information being presented. Conversely, when there is such a natural break, a pause is essential, ideally accompanied by metacomments (see 7.1) that signal unequivocally to the audience that one section has ended and a new one is about to begin (e.g., *so much for the theoretical implications; now let's look at the practical ones*).

Finally, it is important to remember that, while a CP audience is disadvantaged relative to readers, presenters have some tools at their disposal that writers lack. They can employ intonation to differentiate statements from questions and exhortations, to express emphasis and to indicate their attitude towards what they are saying and towards their audience. And, of course, they can make use of body language and facial expression to enhance their message.

A1.2 The purposes

Apart from the audience, the other key factor shaping communications generally is their purpose(s). So what are these in the case of a CP? Heino, Tervonen and Tommola (2002: 128) suggest that they are twofold, as follows:

- "to convey information effectively and to facilitate the listener's efforts to construct an internal representation of the content";
- "to establish or preserve [the speaker's] position in the discourse community", while showing respect for the audience and without "imposing his or her authority" on them.

We will now examine these two purposes in turn.

Communicating information effectively

Here, Heino, Tervonen and Tommola (2002: 128) distinguish three sub-purposes, the first being the need to "organise the presentation adequately". That means selecting the content to include and, given the time constraint, selecting rather ruthlessly. (A tip here: prepare to present for two to three minutes less than the allocated time as actual delivery invariably takes longer than rehearsals.) A few highlights must and will suffice: key findings, say, especially if they challenge existing orthodoxy, an innovative methodology or a previously untapped data source.

Then these key points must be arranged in an appropriate structure. That will typically correspond to the 'research story' metaphor we have used in relation to articles (see 1.2). A CP, too, will have three delineated parts: a beginning, a middle and an ending. The difference, clearly, is that all three must be more compact than the corresponding parts of a written paper. In particular, you will need to keep your introduction as short as possible (especially any attention-grabbing 'hook' such as a snippet from your data, a powerful image illustrating the social context of your research, or a personal anecdote). Listeners may have less need than readers for an elaborate 'map', especially if the CP's structure follows a standard template such as AIMRaD (see 1.1.1). In fact, the best hook of all is actually your highlights – so move on to them as fast as you can (Harinck and van Leeuwen 2020: 15).

At the other end of the CP, your ending is vitally important, being the part most likely to stick in listeners' memories. The standard approach is to restate succinctly the talk's key takeaways, and as always, a trio is rhetorically most effective. Given the huge importance placed on 'impact' these days (Dunleavy & Tinkler 2021), it may also be appropriate to include a sentence or two on that, discussing the broader social implications of your research. If at all possible, the speaker's final shot should be a short, snappy distillation of their overall message – a 'punchline', as it were.

The second subpurpose identified by Heino and his co-authors is to "convey this organisation to the listeners". Unless the overall structure of your presentation is a standard one (e.g., AIMRaD), then some sort of brief 'agenda' will be helpful. Listeners will also require a degree of signposting (see 7.1). It has traditionally been suggested that that needs to be more elaborate than it would be in writing, but as ever it should not be overdone. Perhaps the most important thing is to be alert to the audience's reactions, and if these suggest some confusion, then provide more signposts. What is certain is that signposting needs to be adjusted to the spoken context: see Toolbox A1.1 for some suggestions.

Toolbox A1.1
SIGNPOSTING IN CPs

- **Pointing back**
  In my talk so far, I've taken a look at B / I've been looking at B.
  That concludes what I have to say about C.
  That brings me to the end of my brief overview of the results.
  So now we should have a clear idea of what I mean by A.
  From what I've said so far, I hope you can see that ...
- **Pointing forward**
  Let's turn now to A.
  Now, as I mentioned at the start, I'd like to move on to B.
  Next, I'll turn to the topic of ...
  (Having talked briefly about C), I'm now going to discuss D.

Note the verb forms in the last three items (*I'd like to move on; I'll turn; I'm going to discuss*). Present simple forms (**I move on; *I turn; *I discuss*) would definitely sound odd here.

The last of the three subpurposes under the heading of 'getting information across effectively' is about clarity of language. To achieve this, it is
generally best to avoid sentence structures too complex for your particular
audience to process on the spot. Perhaps even more than in writing, concrete
examples are important, but they must not be allowed to obscure the general
issue, so keep them short and to the point.

In Brief
CONVEYING YOUR CP'S CONTENT EFFECTIVELY

- Pick out highlights: choose a few key points and focus on them
  consistently.
- Cut to the chase: keep your introduction succinct and move
  quickly to your highlights.
- Consider your audience: adjust linguistic complexity to match
  their needs.
- Go out with a bang: finish powerfully.

Establishing credibility

Achieving this second purpose of a CP is done in two different ways. The
first and most obvious one is that speakers will be expected to competently
present state-of-the-art research. You need to show that 'you know your
stuff', that you are familiar with the key ideas, and use the relevant
terminology accurately. Competence is also associated with being well
organised, not just in the way you have arranged the contents of your talk
but in absolutely basic things like the appearance of your slides (more on
that in A1.4) and the way you manage them. These aspects of credibility, we
can safely assume, are pretty universal.

In contrast, the second way of establishing credibility is heavily dependent on the academic culture of particular countries, disciplines and even
individual conferences. Some such cultures demand a high degree of gravitas
from presenters, who may also be expected to accept unconditionally the
authority of those higher up the academic pecking order. That is much less
the case in many English-speaking contexts; and in the UK, while the rules
haven't exactly been reversed, expectations appear to have become very
different. There, presenters are usually expected to show a high degree of

informality both in their general behaviour and in their mode of delivery – virtually irrespective of where they stand on the career ladder. On the other hand, CP audiences expect even very junior speakers to display confidence through the tone and style of their talk. The best bet as regards tone is probably something close to face-to-face communication, without being over-familiar. But what about style?

Even if enlivened in some of the ways we have suggested in this book, a style of delivery that mirrors written academic discourse may not just prove hard for listeners to follow; it will also create a degree of unwanted distance between them and the speaker. To minimise that distance, you must establish a rapport with your listeners by addressing them explicitly or appealing to shared knowledge or experiences (see 7.2.4); in the CP setting, the latter may include other presentations or social events at the present conference or previous ones.

You may be able to show such 'listener orientation' by choosing a snappy and appealing title (see 1.2.2). Such orientation is essential both in introductions and also in conclusions, where an invitation to engage in the post-CP discussion is *de rigueur*. Humour, though often a good ice-breaker, can backfire badly and is probably best used sparingly, and only once an initial bond has been created (Guest 2018: 26). Last but not least, using the story metaphor (see 1.2) to frame your CP as the tale of your own personal research experience is perhaps even more useful than in writing.

Ultimately, though, audience rapport will probably depend above all on how you deliver your CP: that is, how freely and (apparently) spontaneously you talk. The traditional practice of reading from a script may still be alive in some disciplines, cultures or even particular conferences. Admittedly, too, reading can seem attractive to novice speakers, or those worried about the quality of their English in front of a conference audience. However, this temptation is best resisted. For one thing, listeners to a talk may not notice – or choose to ignore – isolated language errors (although repeated errors are likely to be perceived as intrusive or interfere with comprehension). And, what is more, reading your CP will inevitably sound somewhat stilted – and so is likely to hinder rapport.

Preparing a script is not pointless though. Many speakers find it to be an excellent basis for the rigorous preparation that CPs require (even more so if your talk happens to be a plenary). But it must be a genuine script, a text designed to be spoken and received aurally, not a written academic text designed to be 'consumed' in print.

In Brief
CREATING AUDIENCE RAPPORT IN A PRESENTATION

- Give your talk an enticing title.
- Address the audience directly and appeal to shared knowledge and experience.
- Attempt humour only with great care.
- Tell a compelling research story.
- Remember to invite discussion.
- Avoid reading from a script.

A1.3 Language considerations

Earlier, when we discussed the need to convey your CP's structure, we introduced the idea of signposting. Typically, this is provided at transitions from one part of the CP to the next, a position that also offers the ideal opportunity to provide a 'mini-summary' of the point just made, as well as a brief reminder of the one coming up. No rules can be laid down for how to do this; the possibilities are effectively endless. All we can do is provide a small selection in Toolbox A1.2 as a basis for you to build on and as an indication of how spoken transitions tend to differ from their generally more compact written counterparts.

Toolbox A1.2
TRANSITIONS IN ARTICLES VERSUS THOSE IN PRESENTATIONS

Articles	Presentations
As regards manufacturing, ...	■ *Moving through the sectors in their usual order, we've arrived at manufacturing. ...* ■ *OK, that rounds off our discussion of agriculture. So now let's turn to manufacturing.*
This problem has a number of causes.	■ *There are various reasons why the problem I've just described has arisen. They are, first, ...* ■ *But why does this problem arise? What exactly are its causes? Well, one is ...*

Delving inside the talk's individual sections, we can identify another contrast with written articles, this time with regard to the use of linkers (see 5.2.3). Generally, these will be much less formal in CPs. In Toolbox A1.3, we provide some typical examples, again contrasted with their more formal equivalents.

Toolbox A1.3
TYPICAL LINKERS IN ARTICLES AND PRESENTATIONS

Articles	Presentations
however; nevertheless	*but; yet*
in addition; moreover	*also; added to that*
as a result; consequently	*so; that's why; ... and that means*
subsequently; thereafter	*then; next; after that*

Moreover, given that the concept of a 'sentence' is hazy in speech, linkers that in writing may only be used to connect full sentences can be employed much more freely. For example, *in/by contrast* may become *whereas* or *while, admittedly* or *it is true that* may turn into *(al)though.*

That is far from the whole story, though. The differences between speech and writing in terms of establishing connections are complex, and in spoken genres such links are frequently expressed in ways that are certainly less formal but also (considerably) more elaborate. For instance, a reference back such as *This idea points to...* may need to be amplified by introducing a redundant, but really helpful reminder of what 'this idea' was: *This idea – the notion that it is relative differences that matter, not absolute ones – points to ...* Or a list whose items are enumerated in writing simply by *first, second, ...,* may well need to be introduced in a CP by an advance organiser such as *There are three of these varieties, which I will now explain briefly in turn* (for further discussion of advance organisers, see 5.3). Alternatively, a linking word in an article may be transformed, in the CP context, into an entire linking phrase. It is impossible to give any rules about such expressions, so again we provide a few illustrative examples as a source of inspiration (Toolbox A1.4).

Toolbox A1.4
FROM WRITTEN LINKING WORDS TO SPOKEN LINKING PHRASES

Written linkers	Spoken linking phrases
because; since; as	■ *So why precisely does this situation arise? The reason(s) is/are …* ■ *So much for the outcome. But why do things turn out like that?*
yet; however; nevertheless	■ *Having said that, various things actually point the other way, …* ■ *That's far from the end of the story though. The fact is, several other factors come into play.*
and; in addition; furthermore	■ *But there's a further point that must be added; it is that …* ■ *And the list continues. The next point on it is …*

Finally in this section, the need for rapport will demand that you increase your own presence in the CP (see 7.2.4). In other words, whatever your personal reservations about using *I* and the other first-person pronouns (*me, my, mine*) in a written article, you will have to lay such thoughts aside in the spoken context. The same applies to any reluctance to address the audience directly (e.g., *As you can see on this slide …*), and to using questions (e.g., *Why does that occur?*) or imperatives (e.g., *Let's take a look at this diagram*). Finally, as the last example indicates, using *we, us* and *our* inclusively, as a means of binding speaker and audience together, is another common aspect of greater personalisation in CPs.

A1.4 Text slides

Giving general guidance on the use of text slides in CPs is an almost impossible task. Practice certainly varies between disciplines, and constant technological developments affect the way slides are used by presenters and received by audiences. That is why we will restrict ourselves to mentioning some basics of 'presentation craft' and to a few questions of language use.

As regards the first of these, it is an unfortunate fact that even experienced presenters often forget, or ignore a number of these seemingly obvious points.

- The presenter's name must appear on every slide, preferably in the footer area.
- That area must also contain the slide number, to enable the audience to identify and refer back to any individual slides they may want to comment on in the discussion.
- Font sizes must be large enough to ensure that slides can be read easily by the entire audience.

Above all, slides must be easily intelligible to those unfamiliar with the structure and detail of the CP – not just to the presenter. And, naturally, you must guard against having more slides than you can deal with in your allotted time (one slide per two minutes of talk being a rough guide).

Turning to language issues, the fundamental point is the obvious one that the audience can see the text on your slides for a significant length of time. Spelling and grammar errors are likely to stick out like a sore thumb. So to avoid coming across as unprofessional, you must ensure your spelling is impeccable, your vocabulary use precise and your grammar error-free. Apostrophes, quotation marks and brackets must appear in their English form as indicated in Toolbox A1.5, as must numbers and amounts of money. (For the English way of writing numbers and amounts of money, as well as advice on handling bulleted lists, see 2.2.2.)

Toolbox A1.5
GETTING PUNCTUATION MARKS RIGHT

Incorrect		Correct
a leader`s job	→	a leader's job
„excellence“	→	"excellence"
«brevity»	→	"brevity"
‚outstanding'	→	'outstanding'

The next question is clearly how to integrate slides into your presentation. To what extent should you pause to let the audience take the message in without being distracted by what you are saying? In the CP context, extended pauses – even if desirable – are unlikely to be feasible; there is clearly a danger of listeners 'reading ahead' to parts of slides you have not yet got round to commenting on. A compromise approach – and a highly effective one – is to use the facility of PowerPoint & Co to reveal bulleted points one at a time, as you address them.

To end, a word of caution. As Edward Tufte, a leading authority on information design, has remarked: "There are many true statements about complex topics that are too long to fit on a PowerPoint slide."[1] Of course, well-organised and linguistically irreproachable text slides can do much to help both presenters and listeners. Yet, when all is said and done, the slides are the supporting act, not the star attraction.

---

1   https://www.enquoted.com/edward-tufte--there-are-many-true-statements-about-co mplex-topics-that-are-too-long-to-fit-quote.html

Appendix 2
Grant proposals

In many ways, a research grant proposal is similar to a research article, because it too tells a research story. Research funding organisations may provide forms and templates to suit their particular administrative needs, but these are likely to include all the standard elements discussed in Chapter 1. Target audiences also overlap, as most funders send grant applications out for peer review and/or get panels of experts to assess and choose between projects. In fact, the similarities between research grant proposals and research papers are such that many rejected proposals can eventually form the basis of journal submissions.

Nevertheless, there are differences between *telling* a research story in a paper and *selling* it through a proposal. The former merely asks its audience to listen; the latter also asks it to pay. The former's audience consists exclusively of scholarly peers, whereas the latter also has administrators and officials listening in who hold the purse strings and may be gatekeepers in their own right. On a substantive note, journal articles report on completed research, whereas grant proposals are suggestions for projects that have not yet begun. Last but not least, most funders organise the review not as a double-blind process, which is the norm for journals, but as single-blind. That is, the reviewers know who the authors are but not vice versa. This makes sense because with grant proposals, reviewers are asked to evaluate not only the proposal submitted but also the applicant's academic credentials, experience and publications track record.

In terms of assessment criteria, those related to the project's intellectual merit and its research design are generally the same as for journal papers. Where grant proposals differ is that they are also assessed on feasibility, research management and other operational issues. The full list of questions that funding organisations send to reviewers tends to look something like the following.

- Does the proposed research:
  - □ address a timely and relevant challenge?
  - □ make an original contribution to its field?

- Have the research questions/hypotheses been spelled out clearly? If there are several, is it clear how they are related?
- Are the proposed methods appropriate and have they been described in sufficient detail?
- Is the proposed work plan realistic and detailed enough?
- If the project includes several work packages, does the proposal make clear how they are related?
- Can the project be completed in the time envisaged?
- Does the research design take adequate account of any potential gender-related issues?
- Have sufficient funds been requested for staff, equipment and other resources?
- Does the institution at which the project is to be carried out have the right technical infrastructure?
- Have research ethics been addressed appropriately?
- Is there a state-of-the-art data management plan?
- What contingency plans are in place to deal with unexpected events that could disrupt data collection and analysis?
- Does the Principal Investigator (PI) and their team have the relevant expertise to carry out the proposed research?
- Is the research team adequately balanced in terms of gender?

Naturally, every funding organisation has its own application guidelines. While applicants are expected to follow such guidelines scrupulously and play by administrators' rules, they must not lose sight of the nature of proposals as an essentially persuasive genre. Competition for funds is generally fierce, so that proposals cannot succeed unless they stand out from the crowd. Denscombe (2019: 19) lists six things that will help them do that: "originality", "timeliness", "a topic of special interest", "wider application", "precision", and "telling the story". The last two in particular are down to the skilful use of language. The specific challenge lies in making a strong sales pitch without sacrificing the appropriate degree of academic humility. The best policy would seem to be a matter-of-fact, no-frills tone with enough rhetorical devices to persuade the readership of your project's merits. (For further advice on writing research proposals see Punch 2016 and Locke, Spirduso & Silverman 2014.)

Appendix 3
Phrasebank for academic writing

This phrasebank is based on the one contained in Mautner (2019). It inevitably overlaps to some extent with the Toolboxes in the present book, but we feel that it is better to have 'everything in one place' as well. Apart from that, our phrasebank has the strengths and weaknesses of all such lists. On the one hand, it provides a compact overview and encourages variation in use. On the other, the phrases lack context, so often a decisive factor in choosing between them; the list cannot be exhaustive; and its existence could suggest, incorrectly, that an academic text is like a piece of Ikea furniture rather than the hand-crafted construction it really is. And communication is done through whole texts, not through isolated phrases, however common and important these may be.

In order to take advantage of our phrasebank's strengths without losing sight of its weaknesses, we would recommend the following approach.

- Refer back constantly to the authentic extracts in the body of the book since these are at least an entire sentence and often longer, and so offer some linguistic context.
- Increase the range of available choices by making use of other phrase-banks, by far the most extensive of which is the online phrasebank available on the University of Manchester's website (www.phrasebank. manchester.ac.uk), where you can also buy an enhanced pdf version for a modest charge.
- Take note in your English reading, not only of the ideas contained in a text, but also the way those ideas are expressed.
- Improve your vocabulary range by using the synonyms feature now included in good online dictionaries such as the *Longman Learner's* (htt ps://www.ldoceonline.com/dictionary/) or the *Macmillan* (https://www .macmillandictionary.com/dictionary/); but always remember to check the suggestions they give by using a search engine, to make sure there are no significant differences in the way the alternatives offered are used or the contexts they are used in.

With regard to this last point, it is important to exercise the usual caution about the quality of websites, in particular their linguistic quality. Sites that have good quality control measures in place, such as those of well-regarded journals, are more likely to provide useful guidance than blogs or discussion forums to which anyone can contribute.

To end this introduction, here are a few technical details about the phrasebank.

- British English is used throughout.
- The phrasebank is a purely linguistic tool; nothing it contains is to be interpreted as advice on research procedure.
- Standard patterns are illustrated in tables, whereas individual sentences show more creative combinations of words and phrases that have been inspired by authentic examples.
- The phrases making up a single set are listed alphabetically. There is no suggestion that some are better or more usual than others.
- Forms that constitute full sentences are followed by a full stop, even when in practice they would probably form part of a longer, more complex sentence (see 3.1.2). As a result, the full-sentence examples are overwhelmingly short, but this must not be taken as an indication that only short sentences are acceptable in academic texts (see 2.3 and 3.4.2).

Table of contents

1. Introducing academic texts

The	aim intention objective purpose	of this paper is to	analyse … describe … determine whether … discuss … (critically) examine … explore … focus on … highlight … make a case for … outline … present … show …
In this paper, we/I will[1] This paper/thesis/study/book will The present paper/thesis/study/book will			

2. Defining terminology

X is defined as …
We define X as follows: …
By X we mean …
We propose the following definition: …
Our definition attempts to capture the essence of …
This definition allows us to distinguish …
We use the term more broadly to refer to …
(In the literature,) the term X is generally taken to mean …
The term Y tends to be used to refer to …
In this paper, the term Z will be used to refer to …
X has traditionally been used in the sense of …
X has come to mean …
There does not seem to be a generally accepted definition of X.
The meaning of X is contested / the subject of debate.

---

[1]   In this and the following two patterns, the present simple tense can also be used.

3. Indicating a topic's importance

The	cause of X effect of X impact of X origin of X rationale for X relevance of X role of X use of X		has been studied extensively. has been widely debated. has been the centre of considerable controversy. has received considerable attention.
	connection link relationship	between X and Y	
Whether X does Y Whether X has an influence on Y			

Recently, there has been growing interest in ...

The study of X has attracted considerable attention in recent years.

Of late, there has been a great deal of discussion about ...

X has been studied extensively.

Many recent studies have focused on ...

A key issue, therefore, is whether ...

A central question that needs to be addressed in this context is ...

There has been some disagreement about ...

Researchers seem to disagree on ...

4. Identifying research gaps

So far	*little attention has been paid to* *little effort has been devoted to*	*exploring X.* *linking X with Y.*
	relatively few attempts have been made to	*establish a connection between X and Y.* *explore X.* *integrate X, Y and Z.* *link X with Y.* *measure X.*
Previous research has *Most prior research has* *Traditional approaches have*		*been limited to …* *concentrated on …* *disregarded …* *overestimated …* *overlooked …* *underestimated …*
Previous research	*has failed to* *has neglected to*	*address the issue of …* *adequately consider …* *consistently define …* *develop effective techniques for …* *differentiate empirically between …* *find evidence of …* *identify a relationship between X and Y …* *provide a clear account of …* *provide solid support for the hypothesis that …* *provide sufficient insight into …*

5. Setting out a text's structure

This	chapter paper thesis	comprises consists of has has been divided into is divided into is made up of	three parts. three sections.
The paper begins by		briefly reviewing ... clarifying ... describing ... discussing ...	
It then The paper then		examines in greater detail ... goes into greater detail about ... goes on to analyse ... homes in on ... moves on to consider ... zooms in to consider ...	
It ends The paper ends		by summing up the principal outcomes of the study. with (a discussion of the most important results and) some general conclusions.	

In Section 4, we assess ...

Section 5 provides a critical assessment of ...

Finally, Section 6 offers some recommendations for ...

In the concluding section, we also outline how ...

6. Listing and categorising

There are essentially three aspects of this question: X, Y and Z.
The advantages of our approach can be divided into two categories.
That appears to be one effect of X. In addition, ... What is more, ...
This typology of X is based on ...
This classification was first developed by McGrain (1987).
Categorising data on this basis can be problematic because ...
Nowadays, it is usual to divide X up on the following basis.
Formerly X tended to be seen as ..., yet today it is regarded as ...

7. Giving examples

As the following examples	*demonstrate, ...* *highlight,* *illustrate, ...* *indicate, ...* *show, ...* *suggest, ...* *underline, ...*

For example, ...
For instance, ...
X would be a good example of Y.
X is best exemplified by Y.
X and Y are good examples of Z.
If we take X as an example, ...
Take/Consider X, for example.
X is determined by several factors, such as ...
Another example of X is ...
Several factors have been identified, including ...

8. Describing methods

An experiment
This procedure
	was	carried out
		conducted
			to determine
			   whether ...
			to investigate X.
			to see what effect X
			   might have on ...
			to test hypotheses con-
			   cerning X.
			with a view to observ-
			   ing differences in ...

Internet searches Interviews Several tests	were		

A (random) sample
The sample
	was	drawn
		obtained
			by trawling social me-
			   dia.
			from a questionnaire
			   sent to ...
			from households in two
			   cities.
			from the electoral reg-
			   ister.

A case study approach was used to explore ...

A number of methods were used, including ...

The methods used included ...

The questionnaire was designed to elicit the following information: ...

The subjects were selected on the basis of ...

Data were gathered in the period from ... to ...

Data were collected using a semi-structured, interviewer-administered
   questionnaire.

Ethical clearance for the study was given by ... / was obtained from ...

9. Summarising findings and results

As we have seen, ...
On this basis, it can/may be concluded that ...
To conclude, ...
To recap, ...
To sum up, ...
To summarise, ...
The results may be summarised as follows.
Our findings can be summarised as follows.
On balance, the overall impression is that ...
A tentative conclusion at this point would be that ....
Thus, a preliminary conclusion might be that ...
Our results (so far) seem to suggest ...
In conclusion, it can be noted that ...

10. Interpreting findings and results

The results may be interpreted	*as follows.* *to indicate ...* *to mean ...* *to suggest ...*
Our findings	*also suggest that ...* *appear to be relevant for ...* *(do not) confirm the hypothesis that ...* *seem to contradict those of Smith (2019).* *strongly support the view that ...*
In interpreting these findings,	*we must take into account that ...* *we need to consider that ...* *we should remember that ...*

11. Qualifying findings and results

These results Our findings	must be need to be ought to be should be	interpreted with (some) caution. treated as tentative until ...

On the evidence presented, we cannot be certain whether ...
Although exploratory, the findings indicate that ...
While our conclusions remain tentative, the data reveal ...
We must be careful not to overgeneralise the significance of ...

12. Acknowledging limitations

Our study has several limitations. First, ... Second, ... Third, ...
(As we mentioned earlier), the methods used were not suited to ...
The nature of our data did not allow us to ...
We were able to identify X, but could not establish what causes it.
Our focus / My perspective effectively ignores ...
The general validity of this assumption is yet to be established.
The way in which we conceptualise X does, of course, close off some lines of
    enquiry.
We were unfortunately unable to investigate X in any detail.
It could be argued that our sample was not strictly random.
What this study has been unable to demonstrate is ...
What a purely quantitative approach cannot reveal is ...

13. Pointing to further research opportunities

A more detailed analysis *A more systematic approach* *Additional research* *Considerably more work*	*is* *would be*	*necessary* *needed* *required* *useful*	*to assess ...* *to confirm ...* *to establish ...* *to fully under-stand ...*
More sophisticated methods	*are* *would be*		
Future research	*may* *might* *should*	*attempt to clarify ...* *concentrate on ...* *explore ...* *try to ascertain why ...* *try to determine whether ...*	

14. Integrating tables and figures

Table 2.1 *Figure 2.1* ——— *As Table 2.1* *As Figure 2.1*	*illustrates ...* *indicates ...* *shows ...*
As can be seen from	*Table 2.1, ...* *the bar chart, ...* *the table, ...* *the figure, ...* *the line graph, / scatter graph, / scatterplot, ...* *the pie chart / ...*
It can be seen from	*the table/figure etc. that ...*
From the data in Table 1,	*it can be concluded that ...* *it follows that ...* *it is apparent that ...*
A number of patterns *Important trends* *Two main points*	*emerge from the data in Table 1.*
Several conclusions	*may be drawn from the data in Figure 2.* *can be drawn from the graph.*

15. Describing figures

		gradual marginal sharp slight slow steady steep sudden	decline decrease drop fall increase rise
The figure *The graph*	*indicates a* *shows a* *suggests a*		

16. Cross-referencing

See Section 5.2 for	*a brief review/definition of ...* *a more detailed account/discussion of ...*	
As we	*argued* *explained* *indicated* *noted* *showed*	*in Section 5.2, ...*
As	*was argued* *we noted / pointed out*	*in Section 5.2, ...*
As Section 5.2	*explains, ...* *shows, ...*	

More details will be given below.
Further arguments will be presented in the following section.
Later, we will briefly discuss ...
In later sections, we will show how ...

17. Reviewing the literature

There is a	*large* *substantial*	*amount of research that …* *body of literature on …*
A number of *Many* *Several*	*authors* *researchers* *scholars* *studies* *writers*	*have argued/demonstrated that …* *have reported/shown/sugges-ted that …*
Previous research	*has demonstrated/documented/established that …* *has found/indicated/shown/suggested that …*	
In a recent study,	*Smith (2009)* *Smith & Jones (2010)*	*demonstrated that …* *examined X.* *found that …* *investigated X.*
Smith (2019)	*develops a new approach to X …* *draws our attention to … / emphasises the role of …* *identifies the key characteristics of / offers a typology of …* *lists three reasons why … / proposes a framework which …* *suggests how one might account for …*	
According to Smith (2019), *As Smith (2019) has noted,*	*a key question is whether …* *there are three types of …* *the main advantage of X is that …* *these problems derive/result from …*	
Drawing on earlier work by Smith (2019), *Following Smith and Jones (2021),* *Replicating and extending previous work by Smith (2019),*	*I argue that …* *this article discusses …* *we distinguish (between) X, Y and Z.* *we focus on …* *we propose an alternative solu-tion to …*	

18. Introducing citations

> *acknowledge, add, admit, argue, assert, assume, believe, claim, conceptualise, conclude, consider, declare, demonstrate, deny, develop, discover, emphasise, explain, doubt, find, highlight, hypothesise, identify, imply, indicate, maintain, notice, observe, point out, regard, remark, report, say, show, state, study, suggest, suspect, theorise, think, underline, write*

Smith (2009) identifies several conditions which must be satisfied in order to obtain accurate results.

... as has been hypothesised previously (Smith 2009; Jones & Miller 2010).

As Evans has pointed out in several papers (2006, 2008a, 2009), there is a systematic trend towards ...

It has been suggested by a number of researchers that ... (Jones 2008; Miller 2009; Evans & Brown 2010).

Smith (2009) believes that ..., while Jones & Miller (2010) doubt whether ....

Smith (2009) is clearly right in saying that ...

As Jones (2008) rightly observes: "The problem is analytically and morally intractable."

19. Framing critical comments

A word of warning is in order about drawing conclusions based on ...
The notion that ... appears misguided.
This assumption is highly questionable.
It is doubtful whether a meaningful comparison can be made between ...
Some doubts may be raised as to whether X is sufficient.
We should not jump to conclusions about the causes of ...
When examined critically, this approach turns out to be too limited.
The key problem with this approach is that ...
What these accounts fail to capture is ...
Traditional approaches tend to ignore the impact that X has on ...
The main weakness of their study was that ...

20. Guiding readers through the text

First, Next,	let us we will	consider ... define ... look at ... turn to ...
At this point	it is it may be	appropriate to raise the issue of ... important to consider ... necessary to discuss ... useful to introduce ...

We now turn to ...
We would now like to propose a theoretical framework that ...
In what follows, we will concentrate on ...
Below, we will present evidence to suggest that ...

21. Comparing and contrasting

X is	*almost* *exactly* *nearly* *practically*	*equivalent to …* *identical to/with …* *similar to …* *the same as …*
X is not	*exactly* *precisely*	
X and Y are not	*exactly* *precisely* *really*	*at the same level.* *identical.* *similar.*
	exact *true*	*equivalents.*

X	*is radically* *is slightly*	*different*	*from Y.*
	differs	*considerably* *significantly*	

X and Y are	*completely* *totally*	*different.* *dissimilar.*	
X and Y	*share*	*few* *hardly any* *no*	*characteristics.* *features.* *properties.*
X and Y	*have*	*hardly anything* *little* *nothing*	*in common.*
	differ	*significantly.*	

There is a/an	*considerable* *distinct* *interesting* *major* *marked* *massive* *minor* *significant* *slight* *small* *striking* *substantial* *subtle* *unmistakable*	*difference between X and Y.*

Our analysis revealed both similarities and differences between X and Y.
X seems to share a number of features with Y.
It can be inferred that X closely resembles Y.
These results show a notable parallel between X and Y.
Our data reveal a striking resemblance between X and Y.
These characteristics are not shared by ...
A totally different pattern was found in ...
The concept of X is diametrically opposed to ...
X is comparable in size and complexity to Y.

22. Describing causes and effects

X	*affects* *causes* *gives rise to* *impacts on* *influences* *leads to* *results from* *results in*		*Y.*
The	*cause of* *consequence of* *impact of* *reason for* *result of*	*X*	*appears to be* *could be* *is (likely to be)* *was* *may be* *might be* *seems to be*	*Y.*

The following imply a vaguer, perhaps not strictly causal connection.

X	*appears to involve* *has been associated with* *is a key factor in* *is connected to* *is linked to* *may be associated with* *may be attributed to*	*Y.*

23. Hedging

X may be the most important contribution to Y in the past 20 years.
There might, under some conditions, be a tendency for X to ...
From a legal perspective, what tends to be missing from these models is ...
X is typically the norm rather than the exception.
One possible explanation could be ...
By and large, our results show some support for Hypothesis 1.
These findings would appear to confirm the assertion that ...
Smith (2020) has plausibly argued that ...
Generally, the effect of X should be to ...
Relative to previously reported results, these figures seem rather low.
Supposedly, this development began only 20 years ago.
This need not necessarily result in ...
The inference to be drawn is presumably that ...
These results correspond roughly/approximately with our expectations.

24. Boosting

It has been shown that X will always / must inevitably be accompanied by Y.
X has been incontrovertibly shown to predict ...
X can indisputably be attributed to Y.
Our data strongly support the idea that ...
Without doubt, these findings have important implications for ...
It is now beyond any doubt that ...
We can assert without fear of contradiction that ...
In fact, it is precisely that type of behaviour which cannot be explained by ...
While it is undeniably important to ..., it can be absolutely crucial/vital to ...
These results correspond precisely/exactly with our expectations.
There is a clear/definite distinction between X and Y.

List of references

A. Sources of illustrative extracts

Adger, D. & G. Trousdale. 2007. "Variation in English syntax: theoretical implications". In *English Language and Linguistics* 11(2): 261-278.

Alvesson, M. & K. Sköldberg. 2009. *Reflexive Methodology: New Vistas for Qualitative Research*, 2nd ed. Los Angeles etc.

Attfield, R. 2016. "Progress and directionality in science, the humanities, society and evolution". In *Journal of the Philosophy of History* 10(1): 29-50.

Bailey, A.E. 2021. "Reconsidering the medieval experience at the shrine in high medieval England". In *Journal of Medieval History* 47(2): 203-229.

Ballinger, G. 2022. "Representing bodies and bathing machines: Jane Austen's *Sanditon* and Andrew Davies's 2019 ITV adaptation". In *Humanities* 11, 81. DOI: 10.3390/h11040081.

Banerjee, S. 2020. "Writing bureaucracy, bureaucratic writing: Charles Dickens, Little Dorrit, and mid-Victorian liberalism". In *Nineteenth-Century Literature* 75(2): 133-158.

Barnes, S.J. 2020. "Information management research and practice in the post-COVID-19 world". In *International Journal of Information Management* 55: 1-4. DOI: 10.1016/j.ijinfomgt.2020.102175.

Best, K. & J. Hindmarsh. 2019. "Embodied spatial practices and everyday organization: The work of tour guides and their audiences". In *Human Relations* 72(2): 248-271.

Beyes, T. & R. Holt. 2020. "The topographical imagination: Space and organization theory". In *Organization Theory* 1 (2): 1-26.

Bouvier, G. & D. Machin. 2021. "What gets lost in Twitter 'cancel culture' hashtags? Calling out racists reveals some limitations of social justice campaigns". In *Discourse & Society* 32(3): 307-327.

Brigstocke, J., P. Bresnihan, L. Dawney & N. Milner. 2021. "Geographies of authority". In *Progress in Human Geography* 45(6): 1356-1378.

Butler, N. & S. Spoelstra. 2020. "Academics at play: Why the 'publication game' is more than a metaphor". In *Management Learning* 51(4): 414-430.

Byng, G. 2019. "'In common for everyone': shared space and private possessions in the English parish church nave". In *Journal of Medieval History* 45(2): 231-253.

Caserta, S. & M.R. Madsen. 2019. "The legal profession in the era of digital capitalism: disruption or new dawn?". In *Laws* 8(1): 1-17. DOI: 10.3390/laws801001.

Chambers, R. & G. Berger-Walliser. 2021. "The future of international corporate human rights litigation: A transatlantic comparison". In *American Business Law Journal* 58(3): 579-642.

Cheng, A. & P.E. Peterson. 2021. "Experimentally estimated impacts of school vouchers on educational attainments of moderately and severely disadvantaged students". In *Sociology of Education* 94(2): 159-174.

Clegg, S., M.P. Cunha, A. Rego & F. Santos. 2021. "'Open purpose': Embracing organizations as expressive systems". In *Organization Theory* 2(4): 1-22.

Coen, D., K. Hermann & T. Pegram. 2022. "Are corporate climate efforts genuine? An empirical analysis of the climate 'talk–walk' hypothesis". In *Business Strategy and the Environment* 31(7): 3040-3059.

Coffey, S. & C. Leung. 2019. "Understanding agency and constraints in the conception of creativity in the language classroom". In *Applied Linguistics Review* 11(4): 607-623.

Collier, S.J. & S. Cox. 2021. "Governing urban resilience: Insurance and the problematization of climate change". In *Economy and Society* 50(2): 275-296.

Collinson, D.L. 2020. "'Only connect!': Exploring the critical dialectical turn in leadership studies". In *Organization Theory* 1: 1-22.

Daniels, T.P. 2022. "Blackness in Indonesia: Articulations of colonial and postcolonial racial epistemologies". In *Ethnos*. DOI: 10.1080/00141844.2022.2081239.

Das, A.E. 2019. "Health, harm, and the civic body: Medical language in the speeches of Demosthenes". In *Greek, Roman, and Byzantine Studies* 59(3): 340-367.

Delanty, G. 2022. "Book review. Philipp Felsch, *The Summer of Theory: History of a Rebellion, 1960–1990. European Journal of Social Theory*. DOI: 10.1177/13684310221099208.

Dempsey, K. 2019. "Gender and medieval archaeology: storming the castle". In *Antiquity* 93(369), 772-788.

Donaldson, A., N. Ward & S. Bradley. 2010. "Mess among disciplines: interdisciplinarity in environmental research". In *Environment and Planning A: Economy and Space* 42(7): 1521-1536.

du Plessis, P.J. 2021. "Legal history: The point of it all". In *Edinburgh Student Law Review* 4(2): 1-3.

Edgar, V.C., N.M. Brennan & S.B. Power. 2021. "The language of profit warnings: a case of denial, defiance, desperation and defeat". In *Accounting, Auditing & Accountability Journal* 35(9): 28-55.

Elliott, V. & S. Olive. 2021. "Secondary Shakespeare in the UK: what gets taught and why?". In *English in Education* 55(2): 102-115.

Ellis, N., J. Fitchett, M. Higgins, G. Jack, M. Lim, M. Saren & M. Tadajewski. 2011. *Marketing: A Critical Textbook*. London etc.: Sage.

Evans, J.H. 2020. "Can the public express their views or say no through public engagement?". In *Environmental Communication* 14(7): 881-885.

Flaim, M. & A.P. Blaisdell. 2020. "The comparative analysis of intelligence". In *Psychological Bulletin* 146(12): 1174-1199.

Fleming, T.G. 2021. "Why change a winning team? Explaining post-election cabinet reshuffles in four western democracies". In *Political Studies*. DOI: 10.1177/003232 17211049293.

Fox, S. 2021. "Political alienation and referendums: how political alienation was related to support for Brexit". In *British Politics* 16: 16-35.

Fu, J.S. & K.R. Cooper. 2021. "Interorganizational network portfolios of nonprofit organizations: Implications for collaboration management". In *Nonprofit Management and Leadership* 31(3): 437-459.

Gaim, M., S. Clegg & M.P. Cunha. 2021. "Managing impressions rather than emissions: Volkswagen and the false mastery of paradox". In *Organization Studies* 42(6): 949-970.

Gastil, J. & L. Sprain. 2011. "Ethical challenges in small group communication". In: G. Cheney, S. May & D. Munshi (eds), *The Handbook of Communication Ethics*. New York and London: Routledge, 148-165.

Gillig, T.K., J.T. Macary & L.P. Gross. 2022. "Explain, label or ignore? Exploring LGBTQ-parent families' communication about family identity". In *Communication Studies* 73(3): 314-330.

González-Peño, A., E. Franco & J. Coterón. 2021. "Do observed teaching behaviors relate to students' engagement in physical education?". In *International Journal of Environmental Research and Public Health* 18(5): 2234. DOI: 10.3390/ ijerph18052234.

Goodlad, L.M.E. 2021. "The ontological work of genre and place: *Wuthering Heights* and the Case of the Occulted Landscape". In *Victorian Literature and Culture* 49(1): 107-138.

Graham, P. 2018. "Ethics in critical discourse analysis". In *Critical Discourse Studies* 15(2): 186-203.

Gray, K. & S.F. Gray 2011. *Land Law*. 7th ed. Oxford: OUP.

Gross, J. 2022. "Hope against hope: COVID-19 and the space for imagination". In *European Journal of Cultural Studies* 25(2): 448-457.

Grossman, J. 2019. "Towards a definition of diaspora". In *Ethnic and Racial Studies* 42(8): 1263-1282.

Guess, A.M. 2021. "Almost everything in moderation: new evidence on Americans' online media diets". In *American Journal of Political Science* 65(4): 1007-1022.

Guntermann, E. & E. Beauvais. 2022, "The lesbian, gay and bisexual vote in a more tolerant Canada". In *Canadian Journal of Political Science* 55(2): 373-403.

Haire, N. & R. MacDonald. 2019. "Humour in music therapy: A narrative literature review". In *Nordic Journal of Music Therapy* 28(4): 273-290.

Haldane, A.G. & A.E. Turrell. 2019. "Drawing on different disciplines: macroeconomic agent-based models". In *Journal of Evolutionary Economics* 29(1): 39-66.

Harris, J. & P. Leeming. 2022. "The impact of teaching approach on growth in L2 proficiency and self-efficacy: A longitudinal classroom-based study of TBLT and PPP". In *Journal of Second Language Studies* 5(1): 114-143.

Harrison, V., G. Hole & R. Habibi. 2020. "Are you in or are you out? The importance of group saliency in own-group biases in face recognition". In *Perception* 49(6): 672-687.

Hart, C.S. 2019. "Education, inequality and social justice: A critical analysis applying the Sen-Bourdieu analytical framework". In *Policy Futures in Education* 17(5): 582-598.

Heblich, S., S.J. Redding & D.M. Sturm. 2020. "The making of the modern metropolis: evidence from London". In *The Quarterly Journal of Economics* 135(4): 2059-2133.

Howarth, D. & L. Quaglia. 2021. "Failing forward in economic and monetary union: explaining weak Eurozone financial support mechanisms". In *Journal of European Public Policy* 28(10): 1555-1572.

Howlett, M. 2022. "Looking at the 'field' through a Zoom lens: Methodological reflections on conducting online research during a global pandemic". In *Qualitative Research* 22(3): 387-402.

Hyde, J. 2020. "Mere claptrap jumble? Music and Tudor cheap print". In *Renaissance Studies* 35(2): 212-236.

Hyland, K. 2017. "Metadiscourse: What is it and where is it going?". In *Journal of Pragmatics* 113: 16-29.

Islam, G. & Z. Sanderson. 2022. "Critical positions: Situating critical perspectives in work and organizational psychology". In *Organizational Psychology Review* 12(1): 3-34.

Jarvis, L., L. Marsden & E. Atakav. 2020. "Public conceptions and constructions of 'British values': A qualitative analysis". In *British Journal of Politics and International Relations* 22(1): 85-101.

Jenkins, S. & R. Delbridge. 2020. "Exploring organizational deception: Organizational contexts, social relations and types of lying". In *Organization Theory* 1: 1-24.

Jones, H. 2019. "Property, territory, and colonialism: an international legal history of enclosure". In *Legal Studies* 39(2): 187-203.

Jones. S. 2018. "Printing stage: Relationships between performance, print, and translation in early English editions of Molière". In *Early Modern French Studies* 40(2): 146-165.

Larue, L. 2020. "The ecology of money: A critical assessment". In *Ecological Economics* 178. DOI: 10.1016/jecolecon.2020.106823.

Leduc, G., S. Kubler & J.-P. Georges. 2021. "Innovative blockchain-based farming marketplace and smart contract performance evaluation". In *Journal of Cleaner Production* 306. DOI: 10.1016/j.jclepro.2021.127055.

Levy, M. 2020. "Women and the book in Britain's long eighteenth century". In *Literature Compass* 17(9): 1-13.

Lewis, S. 2021. "The turn towards policy mobilities and the theoretical-methodological implications for policy sociology". In *Critical Studies in Education* 62(3): 322-337.

Lipson, C. 2013. "Comparative rhetoric, egyptology, and the case of Akhenaten". In *Rhetoric Society Quarterly* 43(3): 270-284.

Llewellyn, N. & A. Whittle. 2019. "Lies, defeasibility and morality-in-action: The interactional architecture of false claims in sales, telemarketing and debt collection work". In *Human Relations* 72(4): 834-858.

Loges, N. 2021. "Detours on a Winter's Journey: Schubert's *Winterreise* in nineteenth-century concerts". In *Journal of the American Musicological Society* 74(1): 1-42.

MacDowell, J. 2018. "Interpretation, irony and 'surface meanings' in film". In *Film-Philosophy* 22(2): 261-280.

Mackin, G. 2022. "The aesthetic Habermas: Communicative power and judgment". In *Political Theory* 50(5): 780-808.

Mahn, D., A. Lecuna, G. Chavez & S. Barros. 2022. "Drivers of growth expectations in Latin American rural contexts". In *Journal of Entrepreneurship in Emerging Economies*. DOI: 10.1108/JEEE-10-2021-0388.

Maitlis, S. & M. Christianson. 2014. "Sensemaking in organizations: Taking stock and moving forward". In *The Academy of Management Annals* 8(1): 57-125.

Manata, B. & J. Bozeman. 2022. "Documenting the longitudinal relationship between group conflict and group cohesion". In *Communication Studies* 73(3): 331-345.

Maye-Banbury, A. 2021. "All the world's a stage: How Irish immigrants negotiated life in England in the 1950s/1960s using Goffman's theory of impression management". In *Irish Journal of Sociology* 29(1): 32-53.

McKeown, J. 2021. "A corpus-based examination of reflexive metadiscourse in majority and dissent opinions of the U.S. Supreme Court". In *Journal of Pragmatics* 186: 224-235.

McLean, C. 2021. "The growth of the anti-transgender movement in the United Kingdom. The silent radicalization of the British electorate". In *International Journal of Sociology* 51(6): 473-482.

Miller, D. 2022. "Responsibility and the duty of rescue". In *Journal of Applied Philosophy* 39(2): 313-326.

Mishra, P. 2018. "Truth on trial: Law, memory, and freedom of expression in Europe". In *SOAS Law Journal* 5(1): 40-69.

Monteiro, P. & P.S. Adler. 2022. "Bureaucracy for the 21st century: Clarifying and expanding our view of bureaucratic organization". In *Academy of Management Annals* 16(2): 427-475.

Moore, J.E. 2018. "The artist as reporter: Drawing national identity during the U.S. Civil War". In *Journalism History* 44(1): 2-11.

Moore, S., C. Neylon, M.P. Eve, D.P. O'Donnell & D. Pattinson. 2017. "'Excellence R Us': university research and the fetishisation of excellence". *Palgrave Communications* 3, 16105. DOI 10.1057/palcomms.2016.105.

Munno, G., M. Craig, A. Richards & M. Ali. 2022. "Student journalists exhibit different mindsets but agree on the need for truthful reporting". In *Media Practice and Education* 23(1): 55-72.

Neff, T. 2022. "Media and cultural systems: Connecting national news dynamics and the cultures of social problems through a case study of climate change in the U.S. and U.K.". In *Media, Culture & Society* 44(5): 1-18.

Parker, M. 2018. "Employing James Bond". In *Journal of Management Inquiry* 27(2): 178-189.

Parker, M. & R. Thomas. 2011. "What is a critical journal?" *Organization* 18(4): 419-427.

Piekkari, R., C. Welch & D.E. Westney. 2022. "The challenge of the multinational corporation to organization theory: contextualizing theory". In *Organization Theory* 3(2): 1-22.

Porter T., T. Shakespeare & A. Stockl. 2021. "Trouble in direct payment personal assistance relationships". In *Work, Employment and Society* 36(4): 630-647.

Pösö, T. 2022. "Children's consent to child welfare services: Some explorative remarks". In *Children & Society* 36(1): 52-65.

Raw, A. 2021. "Gender and protest in late medieval England, c.1400–c.1532". In *English Historical Review* 136(582): 1117-1147.

Renz, S.M., J.M. Carrington & T.A. Badger. 2018. "Two strategies for qualitative analysis: An intramethod approach to triangulation". *Qualitative Health Research* 28(5): 824-831.

Sanscartier, M.D. 2020. "The craft attitude: Navigating mess in mixed methods research". In *Journal of Mixed Methods Research* 14(1): 47-62.

Sanson, D. & D. Courpasson. 2022. "Resistance as a way of life: How a group of workers perpetuated insubordination to neoliberal management". In *Organization Studies* 43(11): 1693-1717.

Scales, L. 2022. "Ever closer union? Unification, difference, and the 'Making of Europe', c.950-c.1350". In *English Historical Review* 137(585): 321-361.

Schumpe, B.M., J.J. Bélanger, M. Giacomantonio, C.F. Nisa & A. Brizi. 2018. "Weapons of peace: Providing alternative means for social change reduces political violence". In *Journal of Applied Social Psychology* 48(10): 549-558.

Seuren, L.M., J. Wherton, T. Greenhalgh & S.E. Shaw. 2021. "Whose turn is it anyway? Latency and the organization of turn-taking in video-mediated interaction". In *Journal of Pragmatics* 172: 63-78.

Shaikh, A. 2022. "Marx, Sraffa and Classical Price Theory". In *Contributions to Political Economy* 41(1): 65-82.

Shaw, S.E. & J. Bailey. 2009. "Discourse analysis: what is it and why is it relevant to family practice?". In *Family Practice* 26(5): 413-419.

Shimpo, N., A. Wesener & W. McWilliam. 2019. "How community gardens may contribute to community resilience following an earthquake". In *Urban Forestry & Urban Greening* 38: 124-132.

Shipp, L. 2021. "Appointing a Poet Laureate: National and poetic identities in 1813". In *English Historical Review* 136(579): 332-363.

Skukauskaite, A., I.Y. Trout & K.A. Robinson. 2021. "Deepening reflexivity through art in learning qualitative research". In *Qualitative Research* 22(3): 403-420.

Sofaer, J., B. Davenport, M.L. Stig-Sørensen, E. Gallou & D. Uzzell. 2021. "Heritage sites, value and wellbeing: Learning from the COVID-19 pandemic in England". In *International Journal of Heritage Studies* 27(11): 1117-1132.

Spence, M. 2021. "Government and economics in the digital economy". In *Journal of Government and Economics* 3: 1-7. DOI: 10.1016/j.jge.2021.100020.

Sytch, M. & Y.H. Kim. 2021. "Quo vadis? From the schoolyard to the courtroom". In *Administrative Science Quarterly* 66(1): 177-219.

Taylor, E. 2020. "Social categories in context". In *Journal of the American Philosophical Association* 6(2): 171-187.

Thomas, G.M. 2021. "'The media love the artificial version of what's going on': Media (mis)representations of Down's syndrome". In *British Journal of Sociology* 72(3): 693-706.

Tiersma, P.M. 1999. *Legal Language*. Chicago: University of Chicago Press.

Tinsley, M. 2022. "Towards a postcolonial critical realism". In *Critical Sociology* 48(2): 235-250.

Townley, A. 2021. "The intertextual nature of embedded email communication for contract negotiation activities". In *Text & Talk* 41(4): 539-560.

Turner, D.M. & D. Blackie. 2018. *Disability in the Industrial Revolution. Physical impairment in British coalmining, 1780-1880.* Manchester: Manchester University Press.

Wall, M. 2021. "Communication practices in the production of Syrian refugee belonging". In *International Journal of Communication* 15, 5099-5115.

Warner, C., J.N. Houle & J. Kaiser. 2021. "Criminal justice contact and indebtedness in young adulthood: Investigating the potential role of state-level hidden sentences". In *Social Currents* 8(3): 203-228.

Wight, L. & S. Cooper. 2022. "Binge-watching: Cultural Studies and developing critical literacy in the age of surveillance capitalism". In *Continuum* 56: 1-12. DOI: 10.1080/10304312.2022.2060190.

Winchenbach, A., P. Hanna & G. Miller. 2022. "Constructing identity in marine tourism diversification". In *Annals of Tourism Research* 95. DOI:10.1016/j.annals.2022.103441.

Yates, S. & J. Hartley. 2021. "Learning to lead with political astuteness". In *International Public Management Journal* 24(4): 562-583.

B. Other references

Ädel, A. & A. Mauranen. 2010. "Metadiscourse: Diverse and divided perspectives", in *Nordic Journal of English Studies* 9(2): 1-11.

American Psychological Association. 2020. *Concise Guide to APA Style.* Washington: APA.

Belcher, W.L. 2019. *Writing Your Journal Article in Twelve Weeks*, 2nd ed. Chicago & London: The University of Chicago Press.

Biber, D., S. Johansson, G. Leech, S. Conrad & E. Finegan. 1999. *Longman Grammar of Spoken and Written English.* Edinburgh: Pearson.

Bizup, J. & J.M. Williams. 2014. *Style: Lessons in Clarity and Grace*, 11th ed. Harlow: Pearson Education.

Booth, W.C., G.G. Colomb, J.M. Williams, J. Bizup & W.T. Fitzgerald. 2016. *The Craft of Research.* 4th ed. Chicago and London: The University of Chicago Press.

Cargill, M. & P. O'Connor. 2021. *Writing Scientific Research Articles. Strategy and Steps*, 2nd ed. Oxford etc.: Wiley-Blackwell.

Chicago Manual of Style. Available at https://www.chicagomanualofstyle.org/home .html.

Clyne, M. 1987. "Cultural differences in the organization of academic texts: English and German". In *Journal of Pragmatics* 11(2): 211-241.

Cooper, K. 1999. *Tips on Grammar and Style.* Harvard University Writing Center.

Curry, M.J. & T. Lillis. 2013. *A Scholar's Guide to Getting Published in English. Critical Choices and Practical Strategies.* Bristol etc.: Multilingual Matters.

Denscombe, M. 2019. *Research Proposals. A Practical Guide.* 2nd ed. London: Open University Press.

Dunleavy, P. & J. Tinkler. 2021. *Maximizing the Impacts of Academic Research.* New York: Macmillan.

Graff, G. & C. Birkenstein. 2021. *They say / I say: The Moves that Matter in Academic Writing.* 5th ed. New York: Norton.

Guest, M. 2018. *Conferencing and Presentation English for Young Academics.* Singapore: Springer.

Harinck, F. & E. van Leeuwen. 2020. *The Art of Presenting: Delivering Successful Presentations in the Social Sciences and Humanities.* Cambridge etc.: CUP.

Hayot, E. 2014. *The Elements of Academic Style. Writing for the Humanities.* New York: Columbia University Press.

Heino, A., E. Tervonen & J. Tommola. 2002. "Metadiscourse in academic conference presentations". In: E. Ventola, C. Shalom & S. Thompson (eds), *The Language of Conferencing.* Frankfurt: Peter Lang, 127-146.

Hewings, M. 2013. *Advanced Grammar in Use.* Cambridge etc.: CUP.

Hyland, K. 2000. *Disciplinary Discourses. Social Interactions in Academic Writing.* Harlow, etc.: Longman.

Hyland, K. 2017. "Metadiscourse: What is it and where is it going?". In *Journal of Pragmatics* 113: 16-29.

Hyland, K. & P. Tse. 2004. "Metadiscourse in academic writing: A reappraisal". *Applied Linguistics* 25(2): 156-177.

Koopman, P. 1997. *How to write an abstract.* Available at https://users.ece.cmu.edu/~koopman/essays/abstract.html, retrieved 27 July 2022.

Locke, L.F., W.W. Spirduso & S.J. Silverman. 2014. *Proposals That Work. A Guide for Planning Dissertations and Grant Proposals,* 6th ed. London etc.: Sage.

Macgilchrist, F. 2014. *Academic Writing.* Paderborn: Ferdinand Schöningh.

Mautner, G. 2019. *Wissenschaftliches Englisch.* 3rd ed. Munich: UVK Verlag.

Mautner, G. & C.J. Ross. 2021. *Englische Grammatik für Studium und Beruf.* 4th ed. Vienna: Linde.

Moran, J. 2018. *First You Write a Sentence. The Elements of Reading, Writing and ... Life.* New York: Viking.

Murray, R. & S. Moore. 2006. *The Handbook of Academic Writing: A Fresh Approach.* Maidenhead, UK: McGraw Hill & Open University Press.

Orwell, G. [1946] 2013. *Politics and the English Language.* London: Penguin.

Peck, J. & M. Coyle. 2012. *The Student's Guide to Writing: Spelling, Punctuation and Grammar.* London: Bloomsbury.

Pollock, T. 2021. *How to Use Storytelling in Your Academic Writing: Techniques for Engaging Readers and Successfully Navigating the Writing and Publishing Process.* Cheltenham: Edward Elgar.

Pullum, G.K. 2009. "50 years of stupid grammar advice". In *The Chronicle of Higher Education*, 17 April 2009. Available at: http://chronicle.com/free/v55/i32/32b0150 1.html, retrieved 21 August 2022.

Pullum, G.K. 2010. "The land of the free and *The Elements of Style*". In *English Today* 26(2), 34-44.

Punch, K.F. 2016. *Developing Effective Research Proposals*, 3rd ed. London: Sage.

Siepmann, D., J.D. Gallagher, M. Hannay & J.L. Mackenzie. 2022. *Writing in English: A Guide for Advanced Learners.* 3rd ed. Tübingen: Narr Francke.

Strunk, W. Jr. & E.B. White. [1918] 1999. *The Elements of Style*, 4th ed. Harlow: Longman.

Swales, J.M. 1990. *Genre Analysis: English in Academic and Research Settings.* Cambridge, UK: Cambridge University Press.

Swales, J.M. 2004. *Research Genres: Exploration and Applications.* Cambridge: CUP.

Swales, J.M. & C. Feak. 1994. *Academic Writing for Graduate Students*, 1st ed. Ann Arbor: University of Michigan Press.

Swales, J.M & C. Feak. 2012, *Academic Writing for Graduate Students*, 3rd ed. Chicago: University of Michigan Press.

Sword, H. 2012. *Stylish Academic Writing.* Cambridge, Mass. and London, UK: Harvard University Press.

Turabian, K.L. 2018. *A Manual for Writers of Research Papers, Theses, and Dissertations. Chicago Style for Students and Researchers.* 9th ed. Chicago and London: The University of Chicago Press.

Vonnegut, K. 1981. "How to write with style". *IEEE Transactions on Professional Communication* 24(2), 66-67.

Vonnegut, K. & S. McConnell. 2019. *Pity the Reader: On Writing with Style.* New York: Seven Stories Press.

Zinsser, W. 2006. *On Writing Well: The Classic Guide to Writing Nonfiction*, 30th Anniversary Edition. New York: Collins.

Index

BUCHTIPP

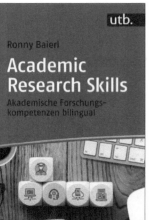

Ronny Baierl

Academic Research Skills

Akademische Forschungskompetenzen bilingual

1. Auflage 2021,
106 Seiten
€[D] 21,90
ISBN 978-3-8252-5698-2
eISBN 978-3-8385-5698-7

Wissenschaftliches Arbeiten bilingual verstehen und anwenden

Forschung ist international. Deswegen ist es bereits für Masterstudierende wichtig, sich frühzeitig mit der Wissenschaftssprache Englisch auseinanderzusetzen. Dieses Buch bietet einen kompakten und vor allem zweisprachigen (deutsch/englisch) Einstieg in ausgewählte Themenfelder der Forschungskompetenz. Die eigenmotivierte Anwendung des Erlernten ist Bestandteil aller Lektionen.

Das Buch eignet sich insbesondere für Masterstudierende aller Hochschultypen sowie für Promotionsstudierende in der Anfangsphase.

UVK Verlag. Ein Unternehmen der Narr Francke Attempto Verlag GmbH + Co. KG
Dischingerweg 5 \ 72070 Tübingen \ Germany
Tel. +49 (0)7071 97 97 0 \ Fax +49 (0)7071 97 97 11 \ info@narr.de \ www.narr.de

BUCHTIPP

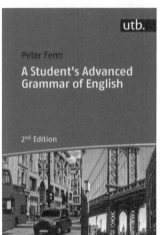

Peter Fenn

A Student's Advanced Grammar of English (SAGE)

2., überarbeitete und aktualisierte Auflage 2022, ca. 600 Seiten
€[D] 41,00
ISBN 978-3-8252-8784-9
eISBN 978-3-8385-8784-4

SAGE is a reference work as well as a programmed refresher course with exercises on the accompanying website, and a structured teaching aid. It serves as a spot-check in specific cases of uncertainty. But it also answers broader queries and provides comprehensive insights into the major structural areas of English. Its concern is not simply grammar, but above all usage.

The second edition has been thoroughly revised.

Narr Francke Attempto Verlag GmbH + Co. KG \ Dischingerweg 5 \ 72070 Tübingen \ Germany
Tel. +49 (0)7071 97 97 0 \ Fax +49 (0)7071 97 97 11 \ info@narr.de \ www.narr.de